COMMUNITY, STATE, AND CHURCH

KARL BARTH's major impact on the world has been through his books, and in particular through *Der Römerbrief* (1919, and subsequent radically revised editions) and *Kirchliche Dogmatik* (1932–   ).

Now a professor at the University of Basel in his native Switzerland, he was successively professor at Göttingen, Münster, and Bonn from 1921 to 1935, in which latter year he was expelled from Germany for refusing an oath of allegiance to Hitler.

WILL HERBERG is graduate professor of Judaic Studies and Social Philosophy at Drew University and author of *Protestant, Catholic, Jew* (Doubleday, 1955; Anchor, 1960).

COMMUNITY, STATE, AND CHURCH

Three Essays

KARL BARTH

With an Introduction by Will Herberg

GLOUCESTER, MASS.

PETER SMITH

1968

The essay *Gospel and Law* was originally published in German by Chr. Kaiser Verlag under the title *Evangelium und Gesetz*.

Library of Congress Catalog Card Number 60–13233

CONTENTS

Foreword   9

Introduction—The Social Philosophy of Karl Barth   11

Gospel and Law   71

Church and State   101

    INTRODUCTION

    THE CHURCH AND THE STATE AS THEY CONFRONT
       ONE ANOTHER

    THE ESSENCE OF THE STATE

    THE SIGNIFICANCE OF THE STATE FOR THE
       CHURCH

    THE SERVICE WHICH THE CHURCH OWES TO THE
       STATE

The Christian Community and the Civil Community   149

Bibliography   191

FOREWORD

This volume consists of three writings of Karl Barth during the most eventful period of his career—the period in which he arose as the conscience of Christendom to speak to the Church and the world of their responsibility in the face of the National-Socialist challenge to mankind. It is my conviction that they still have a most significant word to say to us in the midst of our present perplexities and problems.

The first of these writings of Barth's is "Gospel and Law." It was first published as *Evangelium und Gesetz* by the Chr. Kaiser Verlag in Munich in 1935 as No. XXXII of the series *Theologische Existenz heute*. It records a lecture Barth was to give in Barmen that year, but was prevented from delivering by the Gestapo. As he was being hurried across the border to Switzerland by the German police, the lecture was read in his name by another. The present translation was prepared by A. M. Hall as a study document for the National Conference on Christianity and Law held in Chicago in 1958. So far as I know, no other English translation has appeared.

The second document is "Church and State." It first appeared as *Rechtfertigung und Recht* ("Justification and Justice") in 1938, published by the Evangelischer Verlag, Zollikon-Zurich, as No. I in the series *Theologische Studien*. It was issued in English translation in May 1939 by the Student Christian Movement Press in London under the title "Church and State." The English version is by G. Ronald Howe.

The last of the three works is "The Christian Community

and the Civil Community." It first appeared in 1946 as No. XX of the *Theologische Studien* (Evangelischer Verlag, Zollikon-Zurich) and was included in the volume by Karl Barth, *Against the Stream: Shorter Post-War Writings, 1946–52* (Philosophical Library, 1954), edited by Ronald Gregor Smith.

I have prefixed to these writings of Barth's an introductory essay, "The Social Philosophy of Karl Barth," which I hope will prove of some value in orienting the reader, and have appended a brief bibliography of Barth's works available in English, relevant to the field to which the papers included in this volume belong.

Because the three essays by Barth are taken from various sources, there is considerable diversity in typographical and literary usage, which the reader is asked to make allowance for.

WILL HERBERG

January 1960

THE SOCIAL
PHILOSOPHY
OF KARL BARTH

By Will Herberg

Karl Barth is, beyond all doubt, the master theologian of our age. Wherever, in the past generation, men have reflected deeply on the ultimate problems of life and faith, they have done so in a way that bears the unmistakable mark of the intellectual revolution let loose by this Swiss thinker in the years immediately following the first world war. Whether they have approached him as enthusiastic disciples, as critical inquirers, or as uncompromising opponents, they have all been "Barthians," Barthians even in their anti-Barthianism. If any man has ever put his sign on the thinking of his time, it is Karl Barth, the father of the "dialectical theology."

Barth, of course, comes out of the Swiss Reformed tradition, but the impact of his thought has broken through all barriers of religious confession, national culture, and ideological outlook. It is not without significance that two of the most impressive works on Barth are by Roman Catholic theologians,[1] and that some of his most interesting ex-

[1] Hans Urs von Balthasar, *Karl Barth: Darstellung und Deutung seiner Theologie* (Jakob Hegner Verlag, 1951); Henri Bouillard, *Karl Barth*, 3 vols. (Aubier, 1957).

changes have been with so-called "secular" thinkers, who have looked to him for a new word on the spiritual perplexities of our time. With Barth, theology has become once more a voice to be heard in the fateful dialogue of mankind.

But it would be wrong to think of Karl Barth as merely articulating in classic form the new theological orientation of the post-modern world. He has, in a very significant sense, been its creator as well. His *Epistle to the Romans,* which came as a tocsin call to Christian authenticity in a world that seemed to have lost all sense of the meaning of the Christian message, was indeed a "mighty act"; it was a book, but more than a book—it was a history-making event. It opened a new way, and although Barth was soon joined by others in the great enterprise, it was Barth who launched it, and who gave it its initial direction and character. In Sidney Hook's useful distinction, Barth has been not merely an "eventful" man; he has been an "event-making" man—truly the Carlylean Hero as Theologian.

Karl Barth's main concern throughout his long life has been to proclaim and expound what he takes to be the Word of God. But his life has not been simply one of quiet reflection and scholarship. He has been obliged to do his thinking and writing in one of the stormiest periods of history, and he has always attempted to speak to the problems and concerns of the time. His initial act of theological renovation came in response to the shattering of the modern world in the first world war. Before long, he found himself deeply involved in the fateful Church struggle that was developing in Hitler Germany; with the appearance of his *Theologische Existenz heute!* in June 1933, he emerged as the theologian of the Confessional Church movement, which was attempting to preserve the integrity of the Evangelical Church in Germany against corruption from within and terror from without. His many letters and articles in this period—particularly his letters to his Czechoslovakian, French, English, and American friends—became political forces to be reckoned with in the hard years of war and underground resistance. His leadership in the Church struggle against Nazism made it necessary for him to say something about the Communist totalitarianism that the Soviet power was clamping down upon a large part of Europe in the period after the war; and though his voice now sounded disappointingly equivocal and faltering to many who had become accustomed to look to him for a forthright lead, what he said then, and what he has been saying in the past decade, cannot be overlooked when we consider the plight and the responsibility of the Christian in the struggle between East and West. In this indirect way, a Barthian social philosophy has emerged, and this theologian, who abjures apologetics and desires nothing but to expound the Word of God, has been compelled by circumstances to propound views on society and the state that make him into one of the most influential social thinkers of our time.

It is Barth's social and political philosophy that I intend to examine and comment upon in these paragraphs. My purpose is, of course, primarily to deal with Barth's thought, but in doing so I also hope to show how, by returning to its true origins and recognizing its true nature, contemporary theology is reasserting its relevance to all of human life, man's social concerns included. If I am not able at all points to agree with Barth in his teachings and judgments, I am nonetheless convinced that it is to Karl Barth that we owe so much of our new way of thinking that makes us all, even in our differences, "Barthian" in the larger sense.

I. BARTH'S BASIC THEOLOGICAL ORIENTATION

No one can make any real sense of Barth's pronouncements on social and political questions without some understanding of his basic theological orientation. Here there is a real difficulty: Barth has gone through a complex theological development that has its sharp discontinuities as well as its own inner logic; yet the image of Barth that is still operative in important circles in the English-speaking world is the image of an earlier Barth, which Barth himself abandoned more than two decades ago.

Perhaps it would help to say something about the main phases of Barth's theological development and to indicate the crucial character of the shift that took place in the early 1930s. The Barth with which we in the English-speaking world are most familiar is the Barth of our English version of his great work, *The Epistle to the Romans*,[2] which is a translation appearing in 1933 of the sixth edition of *Der Römerbrief*. This sixth edition is, in effect, not much different from the second edition, issued in 1922; but the second edition, on its part, is drastically different from the original edition of 1919. It is with this first edition of *Der Römerbrief* that we must start;[3] yet we must not overlook the fact that behind the Barth who so startled Christendom in 1919 lies still another Barth, Barth the "liberal," Barth the "religious socialist," a kind of pre-Barthian Barth. As he himself suggests, it was the crisis of the first world war that shook him out of his "liberal" slumbers, and in awakening himself, he awakened the world. Yet the *Römerbrief* of 1919 is a strange document, Platonistic in cast, strongly reminiscent of Origen—in short, quite "un-Barthian."[4] The work was thoroughly revised in the second edition published three years later (1922), and it is here that the Barth of the familiar image really emerges. Within five years (1927) appeared the initial volume of his work on *Christian Dogmatics*.[5] This initial volume was destined to be the terminal volume as well, for hardly had Barth completed it than his thought underwent another drastic shift. It would not be

[2] Karl Barth, *The Epistle to the Romans*, translated by Edwin C. Hoskyns from the sixth German edition (Oxford, 1933).

[3] Barth, *Der Römerbrief* (G. A. Bäschlin, 1919).

[4] See the comments on this first edition of *Der Römerbrief* in Balthasar, *op. cit.*, pp. 71–74.

[5] Barth, *Die Lehre des Wort Gottes: Prolegomena zur Christlichen Dogmatik* (Chr. Kaiser Verlag, 1927).

misleading, I think, to see this shift first clearly expressed in Barth's great work on Anselm in 1931;[6] its outcome was Barth's masterwork, the many-volumed *Church Dogmatics,*[7] which began appearing in 1932.

We have, then, schematically expressed, four Barths: (1) first, the "pre-Barthian" Barth of the "liberal" period; (2) next, the "proto-Barthian" Barth of the first edition of *The Epistle to the Romans;* (3) then the "early-Barthian" Barth of the second edition of *The Epistle to the Romans* (1922) and of the *Christian Dogmatics* (1927); and (4) finally the "late-Barthian" Barth of the *Church Dogmatics* (1932 to date). For our purposes, it is the third and fourth phases that are important, and particularly the shift of theological orientation between them.

What, in essence, was it that Barth said which so startled Christendom in the years following the first world war? It was the word of divine sovereignty and transcendence. This word was directed first against the dominant liberalism, which saw the divine in immanent continuity with the "best" and the "highest" in man's spirit and culture, so that talking about God did indeed become, as Barth was later to comment so caustically, "talking about man in a loud voice." But it was also directed against the so-called "mediating" theology which tried to get away from liberalism and yet preserve the bond between immanence and transcendence by linking the two together and blurring the distinction between them. Against both the liberals and the mediators, Barth insisted on the Kierkegaardian "infinite qualitative difference between time and eternity, between God and man."[8] God is to be reached not by mounting

---

[6] Barth, *Fides quaerens intellectum: Anselms Beweis der Existenz Gottes* (Chr. Kaiser Verlag, 1931).

[7] Barth, *Kirchliche Dogmatik* (Chr. Kaiser Verlag, 1932 to date); English version: *Church Dogmatics* (T. and T. Clark, 1936 to date).

[8] "If I have a system, it is limited to a recognition of what Kierkegaard called the 'infinite qualitative distinction' between time and eternity, and to my regarding this as possessing negative

upward from nature, man, and culture to the divine; God is to be known only through his self-disclosure in his Word. The chasm between God and man that man, from his side and through his own efforts, cannot possibly bridge, God can and does—in his judgment and his grace. God comes to us *senkrecht von oben*—"straight down (perpendicularly) from above"—and creates his own "point of contact" with us, for in us there is nothing that we count on as a point of contact with the divine. Even Emil Brunner, who shared Barth's general orientation but saw some point of contact in man's "capacity for the word," fell foul of Barth's uncompromising criticism at this time.[9] The God to whom the Bible bears witness, Barth insists again and again, is a God who is "wholly other" (*ganz anders, totaliter aliter*) and who comes to us from "above" to shatter and to transform all our enterprises.

It is not hard to see how this word of transcendence came as a cold, refreshing blast upon a world that had lived by a confidence in the essential divineness of its own aspirations and achievements, and had seen those aspirations and achievements come to nought in a cataclysmic eruption from within. This world had lived by continuity and immanence, but now there was no continuity, and the immanence turned out to be an immanence of the demonic rather than the divine. Barth's word of divine transcendence, relativizing everything, absolutely everything, that was not God, seemed to provide a standpoint beyond all standpoints, a stance from which it was possible to live life courageously and resolutely, in a faith that tolerated no illusions. It was, therefore, a word that found a powerful

as well as positive significance: 'God is in heaven, and thou art on earth'" (Barth, *The Epistle to the Romans*, p. 10 [The Preface to the Second Edition]).

[9] See John Baillie, ed., *Natural Theology: Comprising "Nature and Grace" by Professor Dr. Emil Brunner and the Reply "No!" by Dr. Karl Barth* (Bles, 1946).

response in the post-modern mind that was just emerging in the period between the wars.

But Barth's message was, of course, not limited simply to insistence on divine transcendence against immanence and mediation. The God who is "totally other" has nevertheless disclosed himself and come to us in his Word. The Word of God is God-for-us, and the sovereignty of God becomes, for Barth, the sovereignty of the Word of God. By the Word of God, Barth means, in the first instance, the Holy Scriptures as received by the Church, but preeminently the living Word in Jesus Christ. From the beginning, Barth's thought has been radically Christocentric—the self-disclosure of God is self-disclosure in Jesus Christ, the word of God is the word in Jesus Christ, the act of God is the act in Jesus Christ. This thoroughgoing Christocentrism becomes more pronounced and explicit in Barth's later writings, but it must be recognized as present from the beginning (that is, from *The Epistle to the Romans*), and it plays a dominant part in the formation of Barth's social thought.

These few lines do little more than suggest the temper of Barth's theologizing, but they are perhaps sufficient for our immediate purpose. This purpose is to indicate the shift of thought that Barth undertook, or underwent, in the early thirties and that he brought to mature expression in the *Church Dogmatics*. Barth remains throughout the same Barth, the Christocentric theologian of divine transcendence and divine self-disclosure, but there is a difference. And this difference can best be described, I think, as a shift in emphasis, which is more than merely a shift in emphasis. The God who confronts us is still a God who comes to us "straight down from above," but whereas in the earlier Barth (of *The Epistle to the Romans*) the God with whose imminent advent we are confronted is a God who comes in judgment, in the later Barth (of the *Church Dogmatics*) it is a God who comes in grace. The burden of Barth's message in the earlier period is that all mankind, the whole of human existence, all of our highest aspirations and achievements—all stand under a divine *No!* But in the later period, the *No!* of God has turned into a *Yes!* Barth's message is now the message of the "triumph of grace."[10] With the resurrection of Christ, redemption has come; man and the world have been transformed by grace into a "new creation"—to the point, indeed, where sin has become an "ontological impossibility" and faith an "objective ontological inevitability for all" (though what is "ontologically impossible" may have empirical actuality, and what is "ontologically inevitable" may be empirically evaded). Thus Barth turns from what has often been branded as an extreme pessimism to what can only appear at first sight as an extreme optimism. Charles West is indeed right in describing Barth's new way of thinking as "a doctrine of utter grace against a background of utter crisis."[11] It is the failure to understand this shift from the negativity of judgment to the positivity of grace that has made so much of the criticism of Barth, particularly in America, quite irrelevant and beside the point. The Barth who is attacked, even when the image is sufficiently accurate, is a Barth whom Barth himself left behind a quarter of a century ago.

The shift from *The Epistle to the Romans* to *Church Dogmatics* is a shift that involves other aspects of Barth's thinking as well. Barth has throughout followed the "existentialist" formula, according to which "being comes out of doing" (*"esse sequitur agere, esse sequitur operari"*) rather than the reverse favored by the "essentialists" (*"doing comes out of being," "agere sequitur esse, operari sequitur esse"*). This formula means, in effect, that one *is* what he does. This is true of man: "Human being is a his-

10 This is the title of a significant work by G. C. Berkouwer, *The Triumph of Grace in the Theology of Karl Barth* (Eerdmans, 1956).

11 Charles West, *Communism and the Theologians* (S.C.M. Press, 1958), p. 239.

tory."[12] This is true even of God, perhaps pre-eminently of God: ". . . the one free living God, who, in that he is such, has a history, and indeed, *is* a history."[13] Being and acting are not separable and successive; being is implicit acting, acting is explicit being.

In the earlier Barth, this understanding of being and acting leads to a kind of theological "actualism," in which every moment is seen as constituted by the divine action, and there is no immanent continuity in time and history. In the later Barth, however, a kind of objectivism emerges with its own ontological continuity. Where previously judgment shattered, grace now makes whole. And, likewise, where judgment once threw everything into question, grace gives us a certain confidence in knowledge, even in the knowledge of God. Barth's earlier position is one of theological agnosticism: the only knowledge of God of which we are capable is "ac-knowledgment" of oneself as known by God. "As ministers," he says in one unforgettable passage, "we ought to speak of God. We are human, however, and so we cannot speak of God. We ought therefore to recognize both our obligation and our inability, and by that very recognition give God the glory."[14] But the later Barth takes a position closer to theological positivism than to theological agnosticism. Now he speaks of a knowledge of God which is knowledge of an Object into which the Subject has gra-

[12] West, *op. cit.*, p. 226.

[13] F. W. Canfield, "Development and Present Stage in the Theology of Karl Barth," in F. W. Canfield, ed., *Reformation Old and New: A Tribute to Karl Barth* (Lutterworth, 1947), p. 63.

[14] Barth, "The Task of the Ministry" (October 1922), in *The Word of God and the Word of Man* (Pilgrim Press, 1928), p. 186. Other expressions of Barth's earlier attitude are worth noting: "God is pure negation" (*The Epistle to the Romans*, p. 422); "God must never be identified with anything which we name, or experience, or conceive, or worship" (*op. cit.*, p. 331); "We who stand in this [human] world know nothing, are incapable of knowing anything of that other [divine] world" (*op. cit.*, p. 30).

ciously converted himself. "The fact that *we* know him [God]," he says in *Church Dogmatics,* "must mean that, with our views, concepts, and words, we do not describe and express something quite different from himself, but that in and by these means of ours, the only ones we have, we describe and express God himself. Otherwise, without this relationship, under the presupposition of a simple disparity, there cannot possibly be any question of the veracity of our knowledge of God."[15] The God who was "wholly other" and whom we therefore could not know, to the point indeed where any human knowledge of him would be "at once dissolved by the very criterion by which it was created,"[16] has now become a God whom we can genuinely know and "designate." This new capacity may be said to mark the epistemological side of the "triumph of grace," corresponding to the ontological objectivism and continuity we have noted. No wonder certain of Barth's earlier critics have seen in Barth's turn a (to them not unwelcome) return to a theology of mediation.

When Barth was emphasizing the "infinite qualitative difference between God and man," the only theology possible for him was a negative, critical, dialectical theology,[17] in which the word of God emerges "in *diakrisis,* in the decision between revelation and hiddenness," as something we

[15] Barth, *Church Dogmatics,* II/1, p. 225.

[16] Barth, *The Epistle to the Romans,* p. 228.

[17] A classic formulation of the dialectical tension so characteristic of the earlier Barth may be found in the celebrated essay, "The Problem of Ethics Today" (September 1922): "For a definition of *faith* I go to that place in the Gospel where the words are found, 'Lord, I believe, help thou mine unbelief'; and for a definition of *revelation* to a sentence of Luther, 'I do not know it and do not understand it, but sounding from above and ringing in my ears I hear what is beyond the thought of man.' Faith and revelation expressly deny that there is any way from man to God and God's grace, love, and life. Both words indicate that the only way between God and man is that which leads *from* God *to* man" (Barth, *The Word of God and the Word of Man,* p. 179).

know and yet do not know, as something we "recognize" only because we "are recognized in it."[18] But now that he repudiates the "presupposition of simple dissimilarity," he is able to speak of a positive, even ontological theology, in which knowledge of God by analogy becomes possible— not indeed the Thomistic *analogia entis* (analogy of being) which argues upward from man to God, but rather the *analogia fidei* or *relationis* (analogy of faith, of relation) in which the movement is downward from God to man through Christ. Yet however different the analogy, analogy it remains—something quite impossible in a consistent theology of *diakrisis*.

There is no need to carry this analysis much further. The purpose has been not to expose inconsistencies in Barth's thinking—as a matter of fact, his thinking through forty years has been remarkably consistent in essentials—but rather to indicate the nature of the shift that has led him to abandon his first venture in constructing a dogmatic system and to begin again six years later, in 1933, with his *Church Dogmatics*. This shift has its nuclear logic in the movement from judgment to grace, but its ramifications spread through every field of Barth's thinking.

Barth's social and political philosophy, too, has been affected by this shift. Here we have to go largely by implication and inference, since until the middle 1930s Barth's social writings were slight, and never have they loomed very large in the total corpus of his work. Yet they are important both because of the historical crisis out of which they arose, and because they represent the response of a powerful theological mind to a challenge of unprecedented depth and urgency. Let us now turn to what Barth has actually had to say about the problems of society, church, and state, war and revolution, totalitarianism and democracy, with which he has been repeatedly forced to deal through the course of the past quarter of a century.

[18] Barth, *Die Lehre des Wort Gottes: Prolegomena zur Christlichen Dogmatik,* pp. 19, 103.

II. BARTH'S TEACHING ABOUT SOCIETY, STATE, AND CHURCH

Karl Barth's social thinking emerges first as Christian socialism, in the form this movement took in the decades before the first world war. He was at this time much influenced by such men as Hermann Kutter and Leonhard Ragaz, who were preaching the gospel of socialist realization as a religious task. Their thought, by and large, represented a continental, and therefore a rather more sophisticated, version of the Social Gospel. They (particularly Ragaz) strongly emphasized eschatology—the "coming of the Kingdom"—but the Kingdom they heralded was, in effect, the socialist utopia, and Christian endeavor was largely understood as working for socialism. Obviously, this simple gospel could not withstand the impact of the critical-dialectical theology of transcendence as that emerged in 1919, and although Barth has remained a socialist of sorts throughout his life, his socialism, too, became relativized and thrown under the judgment of the divine *No!*

Perhaps nowhere in Barth is the divine *No!* so mercilessly shattering as when it confronts the pretensions of the social conservative, on the one side, and the social radical, on the other. The "existing order" (*das Bestehende*) is denounced as a "new strengthening and defence of men against God," called into question by all the accusations which have been hurled at it from the Book of Revelation to Nietzsche, from the Anabaptists to the anarchists.[19] The "existing order as such is the evil,"[20] but so is the social radicalism that arrays itself against the existing order to destroy it. In fact, "the revolutionary is more overcome of evil than the conservative, because with his 'No' he stands so strangely near to God."[21] The revolutionary, as Charles West puts it,

[19] Barth, *The Epistle to the Romans*, p. 479.
[20] Barth, *op. cit.*, p. 479.
[21] Barth, *op. cit.*, p. 480.

"claims what no man can claim—to be right over against his neighbor. He sets up a new order, which is then just as tyrannical as the old."[22] "The revolutionary has erred," Barth concludes. "He really means *the* Revolution which is the impossible possibility. He means forgiveness of sins and the resurrection of the dead."[23] Only Christ, with his revolution-in-permanence, can overcome the "existing order," as well as the self-divinizing pretensions of the revolutionary.

All this the earlier Barth says with unforgettable force and conviction. But the implication is that all "intermediate" social and political questions lose their real seriousness for the Christian who sees them in the ultimate perspective. And this is indeed what Barth affirms again and again in this period. World history is characterized by a pervasive "monotony";[24] politics and political questions are "fundamentally uninteresting";[25] human society is "either a company of highly individual members from which the crying wrongs that go with such a membership are never absent, or a kind of barracks, ruled by constraint, tediousness, and stupidity, wherein right is wrong"[26] (he is obviously referring to individualism on the one side and to collectivism on the other). While generally supporting the "political and trade-union brands of socialistic workers movements,"[27] Barth and his friends at this time saw political activity as theologically tolerable only when carried on as "essentially a game; that is to say, when we are unable to speak of absolute political right . . . and when room has perhaps been made for that relative moderateness or for that relative radicalism in which human possibilities are re-

[22] West, *Communism and the Theologians*, p. 181.
[23] Barth, *The Epistle to the Romans*, p. 481.
[24] Barth, *Church Dogmatics*, IV/1, p. 307.
[25] Barth, *ibid.*
[26] Barth, *The Word of God and the Word of Man*, p. 166.
[27] Eduard Thurneysen, "Zum religiössozialen Problem," *Zwischen den Zeiten*, 5. Jahrg. (1927), p. 516.

nounced."[28] This is a fine, essentially conservative maxim for a settled society, in which a state based on law (*Recht-staat*) is taken for granted. But what happens when the very foundations of the state and of settled society are called into question, as they are in a Nazi or Communist revolution? Can politics continue to be played as a "game," or has not the game suddenly become a game "for keeps"? To these questions the earlier Barth can give no real answer. His very presuppositions prevent him from facing questions of this sort, since he has developed no way of relating the ultimately serious concerns of faith to the "fundamentally uninteresting" issues of politics.

In Western thinking, there have been two ways in which the political order embodied in the state has been understood and related to the God of faith. The first is the doctrine of natural law. In this conception, which stems from Greek philosophy and Roman law, and has been taken over, though in much modified form, by Christian rationalism, the fundamental principles of social and political life are seen as given in the nature of man. Man has a specific nature, a rationally intelligible nature possessing a well-defined normality of functioning, which is the natural law of its being. This natural law is both moral and political; certain patterns of action and certain forms and structures of political life are required by the very nature of man for its perfection, though, of course, these can be laid down only in a general way, with due allowance for a wide range of historical variation.[29] In other words, the natural-law philosophy operates with the concept of the "natural order." "The natural order," Germino explains in his perceptive study of recent Christian political thought, "is the organization of the human community in a manner conducive

[28] Barth, *The Epistle to the Romans*, p. 489.
[29] An influential modern version of the natural law doctrine will be found in the writings of Jacques Maritain; see, especially, "Natural Law and Moral Law," in Ruth Nanda Anshen, ed., *Moral Principles of Action* (Harper, 1952).

to the fulfillment of the ends proper to man's distinctively human nature. Such an ordering of human relations is an embodiment of the natural law. . . . Natural law demands that the rational element in the human constitution be cultivated, and that it serve as master of the passions. There is thus a hierarchy of the psyche's impulses and faculties, which, if disturbed, results in profound disorder of the soul. There is similarly a hierarchy of goals for the political community, which grows out of and reflects the ranking of ends in man's own being, for the end of the state is not qualitatively different from the end of its members."[30] The natural law derives ultimately from God, and so man has available to him, through the exercise of his reason, an understanding of the God-ordained principles which determine the proper ordering of society and the state.

This is substantially the view held by Roman Catholic thinkers and by many in the Anglican communion, as well as by a number of people without any particular religious affiliation. It obviously assigns a great positive value to the state, which is held to be the highest of human communities and the consummate expression of man's social nature. "The state exists both that man may live, and that he may live a life worthy of man, a life of reason, virtue, and culture."[31] In fact, the state may well be regarded as, humanly speaking, the human-making community.

The other philosophy of the state that has been very influential in Western thought is drawn not from Greek sources but from the Church Fathers, who themselves derived it from the Scriptures, though a Stoic admixture is not to be denied. In this view, the state is evaluated in a much more critical spirit: it is indeed affirmed, and often strongly affirmed, but the affirmation is a curiously ambiguous one. For the state is affirmed as an "order of preserva-

[30] Dante L. Germino, "Two Types of Recent Christian Thought," *The Journal of Politics*, Vol. 21 (1959), pp. 455–86. The quotation is from pp. 457–58.
[31] Germino, *op. cit.*, p. 459.

tion," necessary to preserve society against the disruptive force of human sinfulness. There are three orders of created being, it is held: (1) the "order of creation," defining the order of life for which God created man and which he intends him to live; (2) the "order of preservation," consisting of the forms and institutions of social life made necessary by human sinfulness—that is, by man's proneness to make himself the center of his universe and to subject others to his will—and designed to protect human life in society from the ravages of sin; and (3) the "order of redemption," which mediates the saving word of God to man estranged and lost in his sinfulness. Human society in the sense of community belongs to the first order, since God created man for community and only in community can man realize his humanness. The state, however, is something made necessary by man's sinful urge to self-aggrandizement at the expense of others, and so emerges as an order of preservation. The third order, the order of redemption, is embodied in the Church, though it may be conceived as having aspects that go beyond it.

In this view, which seems to stem from Romans 13[32]

[32] "Let every one be subject to the powers that be (*exousiai*). For there is no power [authority] but of God; the powers that be are ordained of God. Whoever therefore resists the power, resists the ordinance of God; and they that resist shall bring down judgment upon themselves. For rulers are not a terror to those who do good, but to those who do evil. Would you not be afraid of the power? Do what is good, and you shall have praise of the same. For he [the ruler] is the minister of God to you for good. But if you do that which is evil, be afraid; for he does not bear the sword in vain: for he is the minister of God, to execute his wrath upon him who does evil. Therefore you must needs be subject not only for wrath, but also for conscience sake. This is the reason you pay tribute [taxes], for they are God's ministers, attending continually upon this very thing. Render therefore to all their due—tribute to whom tribute is due, custom [revenue] to whom custom is due, fear to whom fear is due, honor to whom honor is due" (Romans 13:1–7). Compare this with a roughly contemporary rabbinical injunction: "Pray for the peace of the government; were it not for the fear of that, we should have

and is certainly to be found in Augustine and the Reformers, the legitimacy of the state depends upon its properly serving its preservative function by assuring justice and order to the community, and upon its refraining from any pretensions to be an instrument of redemption, that is, upon its recognizing its essentially secular character and therefore, if only implicitly, recognizing a majesty beyond itself. Such a state is a divine order, entitled to respect and obedience, not only in "fear" but also in "conscience." But a state that goes beyond its proper calling by "sacralizing" itself, by converting itself into its own highest majesty, and making total claims upon the individual, demanding of him his soul as well as his body, destroys its own legitimacy as a state and takes on the likeness of the "beast out of the abyss" of Revelation 13. It is then not entitled to respect or obedience in "conscience," since it is attempting to arrogate to itself what is properly God's; resistance of some sort is mandatory, though the form and extent must be determined by circumstances. Yet even when the state is obviously unjust and illegitimate, the responsible Christian will think long and hard before he rises against it, since social order is never very secure and anarchy is always lurking around the corner.

It will be noted that this argument for the just state is also an argument for constitutional democracy as the best type of regime. The argument for the state as an order of preservation, in effect, maintains that government is made necessary by human sinfulness and serves to protect society from the destructive consequences of sinful self-aggrandizement. But rulers are surely themselves human beings, and subject to the same temptations that beset other human be-

---

swallowed each other alive" (M. Pirke Abot III.2). —There has been much discussion as to the meaning of *exousiai* ("powers that be"). Barth shares Cullmann's view that *exousiai* refers to the angelic-demonic powers behind the earthly rulers, as well as to the rulers themselves; see Oscar Cullmann, *The State in the New Testament* (Scribner's, 1956).

ings; hence institutional curbs on the power entrusted to them are necessary, and for the same reason—to prevent the inevitable abuse of power that is not in some manner systematically checked and restrained. Calvin in his way understood this,[33] and so did the Puritans;[34] so also did the framers of the United States Constitution, for however far the Founding Fathers may have strayed from the Christian faith, they "believed in original sin" and exhibited a "hearty Puritanism in [their] view of human nature."[35] In the Augustinian-Reformation argument, we may therefore find a significant justification of constitutional democracy;[36] yet we should not forget that there are other types of regime compatible with the legitimate state, and that constitutional democracy as we understand it is actually

[33] "The vice or imperfection of man therefore renders it safer and more tolerable for the government to be in the hands of many, that they may afford each other mutual assistance and admonition, and that if anyone arrogate to himself more than is right, the many may act as censors and masters to restrain his ambition" (John Calvin, Institutes of the Christian Religion, Book IV, Chap. XX, sect. viii).

[34] "The Puritans were suspicious of power in the hands of kings, aristocrats, priests, and churches, [and] by the same token . . . of power in the hands of the people. . . . [The Puritans] recognized that legal power was necessary for curbing unregenerate power, and therefore agreed to civil government, but [they felt that] the exercise of power tended to corrupt men, [and therefore] sought limitation [of power] by means of constitutionalism, the Scriptures and 'politic covenants,' and the dispersion of power. . . ." (H. Richard Niebuhr, The Kingdom of God in America [Willett, Clark, 1937], pp. 77, 80).

[35] "There is a hearty Puritanism in the view of human nature which pervades the instrument of 1787 [the Constitution]. It is the work of men who believed in original sin, and were resolved to leave open for transgressors no door which they could possibly shut" (James Bryce, The American Commonwealth [Macmillan, 2nd. ed., 1889], Part I, chap. xxv, sec. viii).

[36] This is the rationale of constitutional democracy presented by Reinhold Niebuhr in his influential work, The Children of Light and the Children of Darkness: A Vindication of Democracy and a Critique of Its Traditional Defence (Scribner's, 1944).

possible only under certain historical conditions, which are by no means always present.

In any case, the Augustinian-Reformation view of the state as an order of preservation differs, and differs radically, from the natural law philosophy: in the latter, the state is held to be the very expression of human nature in its essential goodness, while in the former it is regarded as the "greatest of all reflections upon human nature" in its ambiguity and sinfulness.[37]

Karl Barth has been able to accept neither of these views. The natural law doctrine is obviously excluded, since it presupposes not only a broad natural "point of contact" between the divine and the human but also the substantial integrity of human nature, human reason, and the cosmic order; in other words, it appears to ignore entirely the pervasiveness of sin and the fallenness of creation. But neither can Barth make the Augustinian-Reformation doctrine his own, for this doctrine seems to him unduly to separate creation from redemption, and therefore to falsify the radically Christocentric character of the Christian faith. He does not hesitate to criticize his own Reformed tradition on this score, as well as on other matters more directly germane to his central theological concern.

Barth does not deny that men, as human beings in history, share certain moral and social principles, and that these may in some way be referred to as natural law. But he insists that this is not the way for the Church or the

---

[37] "It may be a reflection on human nature that such [constitutional] devices should be necessary to control the abuses of government. But what is government itself but the greatest of all reflections on human nature? If men were angels, no government would be necessary. If angels were to govern men, neither external nor internal controls on government would be necessary. In framing of a government which is to be administered by men over men, the greatest difficulty lies in this: you must first enable the government to control the governed, and in the next place oblige it to control itself" (*The Federalist*, No. LI, by James Madison or Alexander Hamilton).

Christian to speak: the Church and the Christian must speak solely and exclusively out of the Word of God. Nor, on the other side, does he deny that the state does serve a preservative function; he, in fact, often stresses it. But again he insists that this is not the way for the Church or the Christian to speak, in terms simply of the "first article" (of the Apostles' Creed): the Church and the Christian must speak solely and exclusively out of Jesus Christ who is the Word of God. But, concretely and on the level of political reality, how may one do so? Here Barth's answer is by no means simple and unequivocal.

In his earlier period, no answer seemed necessary since the whole burden of Barth's teaching at the time was to place the political order, whether conservative or radical, under judgment as part of *das Bestehende* ("the existing order"); from this standpoint, no discriminations were required. With the rise of the Nazi power, however, such an attitude became increasingly impossible. At first, Barth's opposition to the Hitler regime was, as we shall see, an opposition not to the National-Socialist state or society, but to the interference of the new regime in Church affairs and to the theological corruptions it was helping to introduce into the life of the Church. But as the struggle became sharper, and Barth found himself expelled from Germany and back in Switzerland, a very different line emerged. He now begins to talk about Nazism in a new way, and to develop a new doctrine about the "righteous" state and the responsibility of the Church.

But perhaps not entirely new. Hints of it are to be found in the first and subsequent editions of *The Epistle to the Romans*. It is stated explicitly, though only tangentially, in *Rechtfertigung und Recht* (English version: *Church and State*), which appeared in 1937.[38] The full formulation of the new doctrine, however, came with *Christengemeinde*

[38] Barth, *Rechtfertigung und Recht* (*Theologische Studien,* No. I. Evangelischer Verlag, 1938). English translation: *Church and State*. S.C.M. Press, 1939. See below, pp. 101–48.

und Bürgergemeinde (English version: *The Christian Community and the Civil Community*) in 1946, immediately upon the conclusion of the war.[39]

This later Barthian doctrine of the state is, in its developed form, Christocentric indeed, but Christocentric in a very special way. The authority of the state is seen as "included in the authority of Jesus Christ,"[40] as "an image of him whose Kingdom will be a kingdom of peace without frontiers and without end."[41] In fact, the entire teaching is a teaching that hinges upon a correspondence between what is "above" with what is "below," between the "heavenly *polis*" and the "earthly *polis*."[42] The state, Barth insists, must be seen "as an allegory, as a correspondence and an analogue to the Kingdom of God which the Church preaches and believes in";[43] indeed, it *is* the Kingdom of God in "an external, relative, and provisional embodiment."[44] Political action is to be guided by this criterion: "Among the political possibilities open at any particular moment, it [the Church] will choose those which most suggest a correspondence to, an analogy and a reflection of, the content of its own faith and gospel."[45]

Barth is not content with a general statement of his theory of correspondence; he works it out in great detail, and it is in this detailed elaboration, perhaps, that the

[39] Barth, *Christengemeinde und Bürgergemeinde* (*Theologische Studien No. XX.* Evangelischer Verlag, 1946). English translation: "The Christian Community and the Civil Community," in Barth, *Against the Stream: Shorter Post-War Writings, 1946–1952* (Philosophical Library, 1954). See below, pp. 149–89.

[40] Barth, *Church and State*, p. 71; see below, p. 140.

[41] Barth, *op. cit.*, p. 85; see below, p. 148.

[42] Barth, *op. cit.*, p. 61; see below, p. 135.

[43] Barth, "The Christian Community and the Civil Community," in *Against the Stream*, p. 32; see below, p. 169. "Allegory" is not an accurate rendering of the German *Gleichnis*; it should be something like "similitude."

[44] Barth, *op. cit.*, p. 20; see below, p. 154.

[45] Barth, *op. cit.*, p. 34; see below, p. 170.

theory can perhaps be tested. There are twelve such areas of elaboration to which Barth calls particular attention, and it might prove helpful to present them in his own words:

1. The Church is based on the knowledge of the one eternal God, who as such became man and thereby proved himself a neighbor to man, by treating him with compassion (Luke 10:36 f.). The inevitable consequence is that in the political sphere the Church will always and in all circumstances be interested primarily in human beings, and not in some abstract cause or order. . . . Man has not to serve causes; causes have to serve man.[46]

2. The Church is witness of the divine justification. . . . This means that the Church will always be found where the order of the state is based on a commonly acknowledged law, from submission to which no one is exempt and which also provides equal protection for all.[47]

3. The Church is witness of the fact that the Son of Man came to seek and save the lost. And this implies that —casting all false impartiality aside—the Church must concentrate on the lower and lowest levels of human society. . . . The Church must stand for social justice in the political sphere.[48]

4. The Church is the fellowship of those who are freely called by the Word of grace and the Spirit and love of God to be the children of God. Translated into political terms, this means that the Church affirms as a basic right, which every citizen must be guaranteed by the state, the freedom to carry out his decisions in the politically lawful sphere, according to his own insight and choice, and therefore independently, and the freedom to live in certain spheres (the family, education, art, science, religion, culture), safeguarded but not regulated

46 Barth, *op. cit.*, pp. 34–35; see below, pp. 171–72.
47 Barth, *op. cit.*, p. 35; see below, p. 172.
48 Barth, *op. cit.*, p. 36; see below, p. 173.

by law. The Church will not in all circumstances withdraw from and oppose what may be practically a dictatorship, that is, a partial and temporary limitation of these freedoms, but it will certainly withdraw from and oppose any out-and-out dictatorship such as the totalitarian state.[49]

5. The Church is the fellowship of those who, as members of the one Body of the one Head, are bound and committed to this Lord of theirs and therefore to no other. It follows that the Church will never understand and interpret political freedom and the basic law which the state must guarantee to the individual citizen other than in a sense of the basic duty of responsibility which is required of him. . . . Thus the Christian approach surpasses both individualism and collectivism.[50]

6. As the fellowship of those who live in one faith, under one Lord, on the basis of a Baptism in one Spirit, the Church must and will stand for the equality of the freedom and responsibility of all adult citizens, in spite of its sober insight into the variety of human needs, abilities, and tasks.[51]

7. Since the Church is aware of the variety of the gifts and tasks of the one Holy Spirit in its own sphere, it will be alert and open in the political sphere to the need to separate the different functions and "powers."[52]

8. The Church lives from the disclosure of the true God and his revelation from him as the Light. . . . The inevitable political corollary of this is that the Church is the sworn enemy of all secret policies and secret diplomacy.[53]

9. The Church sees itself established and nourished by the free Word of God. . . . And in its own sphere,

[49] Barth, *op. cit.*, pp. 36–37; see below, pp. 173–74.
[50] Barth, *op. cit.*, p. 37; see below, p. 174.
[51] Barth, *op. cit.*, p. 38; see below, p. 175.
[52] Barth, *op. cit.*, p. 38; see below, p. 175.
[53] Barth, *op. cit.*, p. 39; see below, p. 176.

the Church believes that the human word is capable of being the free vehicle and mouthpiece of this free Word of God. By a process of analogy, it has to risk attributing a positive and constructive meaning to the free human word in the political sphere. . . . With all its strength, it will be on the side of those who refuse to have anything to do with the regimentation, controlling, and censoring of public opinion.[54]

10. As disciples of Christ, the members of his Church do not rule; they serve. In the political community, therefore, the Church can only regard all ruling that is not primarily a form of service as a diseased and never as a normal condition.[55]

11. Since the Church is ecumenical (catholic) by virtue of its very origin, it resists all abstract local, regional, and national interests in the political sphere. It will always seek to serve the best interests of the particular city and place where it is stationed. But it will never do this without at the same time looking out beyond the city walls.[56]

12. The Church knows God's anger and judgment, but it also knows that his anger lasts but for a moment, while his mercy is for eternity. The political analogy of this truth is that violent solutions of conflicts in the political community—from police measures to law court decisions, from the armed rising against a regime that is no longer worthy of or equal to its task (in the sense of a revolt undertaken not to undermine but to restore the lawful authority of the state) to the defensive war against an external threat to the lawful state—must be approved, supported, and if necessary even suggested by the Christian community. . . . On the other hand, it can only regard violent solutions of any conflict as an *ultima ratio regis*. It will approve and support them only when

[54] Barth, *op. cit.*, pp. 39–40; see below, pp. 176–77.
[55] Barth, *op. cit.*, p. 40; see below, p. 177.
[56] Barth, *op. cit.*, pp. 40–41; see below, p. 178.

they are for the moment the ultimate and only possibility available.[57]

What shall we make of this view of the Christian understanding of the state? It is certainly strange, but its strangeness should not impel us simply to dismiss it without examination. We must take seriously Barth's intention to speak, even in this field, from out of the Church and its witness to Jesus Christ, without allowing any other voice to interfere. And we cannot but admire the ingenuity with which he carries through his analogy of "above" and "below" at every point.

We may be impressed, but are we convinced? Hardly! The objections to the Barthian teaching on analogy are so obvious and so compelling that we are hard put to it to understand why Barth himself has not seen them from the very start.

Is it not obvious, for example, that his method of analogy is a most arbitrary one, far more so than the natural-law argument which he castigates as "Janus-faced"? Most of the conclusions Barth reaches commend themselves to us, but is it not evident on the face of it that very different conclusions could just as easily have been drawn from the same premises by the same method? We cannot but agree with Emil Brunner when he points out against Barth that "anything and everything can be derived from the same principle of analogy: a monarchy just as well as a republic (Christ the King), a totalitarian state just as much as a state with civil liberties (Christ the Lord of all, man a servant, indeed a slave, of Jesus Christ)."[58] Is it possible to doubt that what Barth is really doing is adjusting his "Christological" arguments to conclusions *already* reached *on other grounds*? In other words, Barth takes the values of a pluralistic constitutional democracy as given, ingen-

[57] Barth, *op. cit.*, p. 41; see below, pp. 178–79.
[58] Emil Brunner, *The Christian Doctrine of Creation and Redemption* (Westminster, 1952), p. 319.

iously discovers more or less plausible counterparts for them in the realm of Church and Gospel, and then proceeds to "derive" the former from the latter.[59] A procedure neither plausible nor particularly fruitful, it would seem.

But the difficulty goes deeper. Where can warrant be found for this method of analogy or correspondence between the "above" and the "below"? Certainly not in the Bible. Is it not more at home in the Platonic-Origenistic context of the first edition of *The Epistle to the Romans,* with its "emblems" and "archetypes," than in the actualistic "event" theology of the mature Barth, with its emphasis on the God who acts in history? We cannot help but regard the correspondence doctrine, however seriously Barth takes it and however ingeniously he works it out, not only as unconvincing but also as pretty much out of line with the main trend of his theological work.

As a matter of fact, what Barth actually depends upon in much of his political thinking is the familiar Augustinian-Reformation doctrine of the state as an order of preservation. This is true even, and especially, of the very work (*The Christian Community and the Civil Community*) in which the correspondence doctrine is developed in the most elaborate form. "The Christian community [the Church]," Barth here declares, "is aware of the need for the civil community [the state]. . . . For—because it knows of the Kingdom and grace of God—it knows of man's presumption and the plainly destructive consequences of man's presumption. It knows how dangerous man is and how endangered by himself. It knows him as a sinner, that is, as a being who is always on the point of opening the sluices through which, if he were not checked in time, chaos and nothingness would break in and bring human time to an end. . . . [The

[59] Gill asks quite pertinently: "Is it merely a coincidence that the Christological analogies which he [Barth] deduces are exactly what is the content of natural law today?" (Theodore Alexander Gill, *Recent Protestant Political Theory* [privately printed, 1953], p. 112).

state] is based on an ordinance of God which is intended for a 'world not yet redeemed,' in which sin and the danger of chaos have to be taken into account. . . . [It] is founded on the gracious ordinance of God by which man is preserved and his sin and crime confined."[60] Had Barth been willing to make this teaching his nuclear doctrine, he might have derived all of his conclusions in a much more secure and Biblically true manner. But then he might not have been able so easily to insert the state into the order of redemption, which is apparently what he feels his Christocentric emphasis requires him to do.

Barth's discussion of the state takes place in close connection with his reflections on the Church. He agrees substantially with Cullmann's picture of the Christian community (*ekklesia*) and the civil community (*polis*) as both within and under the kingship of Christ, the Church constituting the "inner circle" within the "wider circle" of the world.[61] The Church's primary calling is to preach the saving word of God, but it also has its responsibility to the state—to pray for it, to intercede on its behalf, to speak to it in encouragement and admonition from out of its witness to Jesus Christ. For—and this is what constitutes the "relation between the two realms"—"apart from the Church, nowhere is there any fundamental knowledge of the reasons which make the state legitimate and necessary."[62] Indeed, "the existence of the Christian community is [itself] political. . . . The object of the promise and the hope in which the Christian community has its eternal goal consists . . . in the *polis* built by God . . . in a heavenly *politeuma* (Philippians 3:20) . . . in the *basileia* of God. . . . Bearing all this in mind, we are entitled to regard the existence of the Christian community as of ultimate and supreme po-

[60] Barth, "The Christian Community and the Civil Community," in *Against the Stream*, pp. 20, 31, 28; see below, pp. 154–55, 168, 164.

[61] Barth, *op. cit.*, p. 20; see below, p. 155.

[62] Barth, *Church and State*, p. 70; see below, p. 140.

litical significance."[63] More, we are entitled to see in this relation the analogy or correspondence by which the state is to be understood: "The light which falls from the heavenly *polis* upon the earthly *ekklesia* is reflected in the light which illuminates the earthly *polis* from the earthly *ekklesia* through their mutual relation."[64] The Church is thus quite central in Barth's political philosophy, and it was his concern over the Church that first led Barth to re-enter the political arena after his interest in social questions had gone "underground for a period."[65]

III. BARTH'S ENCOUNTER WITH NATIONAL-SOCIALISM

Barth himself has pointed out on several occasions that his opposition to National-Socialism in the first years after Hitler's accession to power was not an opposition to the new regime or even to the totalitarian state, but rather to the confusion and corruption Nazism was bringing into the Church. Late in 1933 he explained: "I am withstanding a theology that is today seeking refuge in National-Socialism, not the National-Socialist ordering of state and society,"[66] and this remained his position for some time. What he was fighting against was essentially the "German Christian" ideology, which closely identified "Germanism" with Christianity (*Volkstum und Evangelium*) and saw in the Nazi revolution an act of divine redemption and a source of divine revelation. Against this heresy, which reached far beyond the confines of the "German Christian" movement, Barth raised a voice that found expression in the celebrated Barmen Declaration: "The inviolable foundation of the German Evangelical Church is the Gospel of Jesus Christ, as it

[63] Barth, "The Christian Community and the Civil Community," in *Against the Stream*, p. 19; see below, p. 154.

[64] Barth, *Church and State*, p. 61; see below, p. 135.

[65] West, *Communism and the Theologians*, p. 184.

[66] Barth, *Die Kirche Jesu Christi* (*Theologische Existenz heute, No. V*. Chr. Kaiser Verlag, 1933).

is witnessed to by the Holy Scriptures and as it comes to light anew in the Confessions of the Reformation. . . . We reject the false doctrine that the Church can and must acknowledge as a source of its proclamation, beside and in addition to this one word of God, other events, powers, forms, and truths as the revelation of God."[67] It was this purely theological stand for authentic Christian faith that first arrayed Barth against the new regime. Indeed, his initial blast against Nazism—*Theologische Existenz heute!*, completed on June 25, 1933[68]—was precisely such a warning of the danger of "losing our theological existence," followed by a sharp criticism of the "German Christians" and the somewhat similar Young-Reformation movement, and concluding with a resounding call to the Church: "Today, we must protect and preserve our theological existence better than yesterday we were able to do!"

Enveloped in this fundamental confrontation between Barth and the new Nazi regime was a series of conflicts on specific issues of Church life and practice. The most important was opposition to the Nazi efforts to "co-ordinate" the Evangelical Church by reorganizing it under the direction of Reich-Bishop Ludwig Müller; as early as August 1934, the Confessional Church movement openly proclaimed: "Obedience to this Church government is disobedience to God."[69] Then, too, there was resistance to the "Aryan paragraph" as applied to the Church, according to which Christians of Jewish origin were to be excluded from the Christian community and its responsible leadership. In fact, for Barth, anti-Semitism soon became the crucial theological

[67] Appeal and Resolution of the Confessional Synod of the German Evangelical Church in Wuppertal-Barmen, May 29–31, 1934.

[68] Barth, *Theologische Existenz heute!* (*Theologische Existenz heute, No. I.* Chr. Kaiser Verlag, 1933).

[69] Declaration Read at the Meeting on Sunday, August 12, 1934, at the Garmenkirche, Barmen, before 1,800 Members of the Barmen Confessional Church.

issue. It was through its anti-Semitism that National-Social-ism revealed itself to be a "basically anti-Christian counter-church." "The really decisive Biblical-theological ground for this assertion," Barth later explained, "is to be found not in the various anti-Christian asseverations and actions of National-Socialism, but in the thing that has been so agitating us these past few weeks, namely, its anti-Semitism in principle. . . . Here the Christian Church is attacked at its very root and threatened with death. . . . Anti-Semitism is sin against the Holy Spirit. For anti-Semitism means re-jection of the grace of God."[70]

During these first years—in fact, well into 1935—the strug-gle was, for Barth, an intra-Church struggle, and his appeal was for theological authenticity and renewal. He did not shrink from the most forthright opposition where opposition was required—did he not in fact virtually challenge Hitler on July 22, 1933, with an address on the eve of the fateful Church elections, urging a stand precisely the opposite of what Hitler was demanding in a great national broadcast that very hour?—but neither did he see the necessity of broadening the struggle into a confrontation all along the line. That was to come later. For the moment, his message was the message of his first pronouncement that had be-come so widely influential, *Theologische Existenz heute!* "We are called upon," he steadfastly repeated, "to serve this people with the Word of God. . . . It is the nature of the message that it can neither be subordinated to, or co-ordinated with, any other concern, however urgent. . . . I maintain that the Evangelical Church ought rather to per-mit itself to be thinned down till it remain a tiny group in the catacombs than make a pact, even a covert pact, with

[70] Barth, "Die Kirche und die politische Frage von heute" (1938), in Barth, *Eine Schweizer Stimme 1938–1945* (Evan-gelischer Verlag, 1945), pp. 87, 88–90. An English translation, *The Church and the Political Problem of Our Day* (Hodder and Stoughton, 1939) exists, but I have not had access to it.

this doctrine [that sees in the Nazi revolution another source of grace and revelation]."[71]

All this time, it should be remembered, there was no thought of challenging the Nazi state as a legitimate state, or indeed as a divine order in the sense of Romans 13. The Barmen Declaration (May 1934), in its fifth article, under the rubric, "Fear God; honor the King" (I Peter 2:17), had testified: "Scripture tells us that, in the as yet unredeemed world in which the Church too exists, the state has by divine appointment the task of maintaining law and peace, by the fullest exercise of human insight and human capacity, by means of the threat and use of force. With gratitude and reverence toward God, the Church acknowledges the benefit of this order which he has appointed." To be sure, it had included a qualification—a rejection of the "false doctrine that the state should or can go beyond its special task and become the sole and total order of human life, thus fulfilling also the Church's vocation." But for the time being this qualification, though big with meaning, remained latent.

Toward the end of 1934, as a professor at Bonn, Barth was required to take the oath of allegiance to Adolf Hitler. He was ready to do so if only it were understood that his allegiance to Hitler was limited by his higher loyalty to God; but this the government refused. For the next eight months the case made its confused rounds in the German courts. Finally, in June 1935, the decision came. Barth was dismissed, left Germany, and was at once called to the University of Basel. The Reich government thereupon forbade German students to attend Barth's lectures there.

From this point on, Barth's attitude began to change. "One week after his dismissal from Bonn," Theodore Gill points out, "he [Barth] was writing with considerable impatience about the Church—even the *Bekenntniskirche* [Confessional Church]—which persisted in accepting the

[71] Barth, *Theologische Existenz heute!*, p. 17.

situation assigned it by the Third Reich, persisted in praying for the divinely ordained government, and, where lies and injustice were elevated to the level of principle, persisted in being satisfied to pray for the eventual release from tyranny."[72] Such a Church, Barth said, "has no heart for the millions of the unjustly persecuted . . . [and] has not yet found a single word to say to the simplest question of public legality. She speaks, if she speaks at all, only of her own affairs. She acts even yet in the fiction that the present state confronts her as a lawful state in the sense of Romans 13. . . ." And he adds: "It will always be a painful recollection for me that I myself, in the last two years, have not been more powerfully behind the direction we now must go."[73] Barth was determined to make up for lost time.

In the very midst of these events, Barth published his *Gospel and Law*,[74] which, in effect, forms the theological point of departure for the new line. The emphasis now shifted from the radical criticism of society, culture, and ethics to a positive message which vindicates the law as a manifestation of divine grace. Gospel and law are intimately related, indeed organically united, as content and form. To "know" God means to keep his commandments;[75] God is Lord, and the Church must ever testify to his Lordship. The Church's proclamation must become a "prophetic witness for the will of God against all of men's sinful presumption, against all their lawlessness and unrighteousness."[76] God's grace converts judgment into justification, but it also establishes justice. There is very little direct po-

[72] Gill, *Recent Protestant Political Theory*, p. 95.

[73] From a letter to a German pastor, in Fritz Lieb, *Christ und Antichrist im Dritten Reich* (Éditions du Carrefour, 1936); quoted by Gill, *op. cit.*, pp. 95–96.

[74] Barth, *Evangelium und Gesetz* (*Theologische Existenz heute, No. XXXII.* Chr. Kaiser Verlag, 1935). For an English translation, see below, pp. 71–100.

[75] Barth, *op. cit.*; references will be to the translation in this volume: see below, p. 79, referring to I John 2:3–4.

[76] Barth, *op. cit.*; see below, p. 80.

litical comment in this address, which Barth had prepared for delivery at Barmen, but had to have someone else read it since he himself was just then being escorted out of Germany by the Gestapo. Yet there is one glancing reference not without significance: among the "falsifications" of the law, Barth lists an example that has arisen "in these recent troubled times": the "*Volksnomoi*" ['people's laws'] so happily invented. . . ."[77] This was the time when "people's justice" in Germany, like "proletarian justice" in Russia, had become the slogan under which all the protections of custom and law were being contemptuously trampled under foot.

Rechtfertigung und Recht (English version: *Church and State*), published in the fateful year 1938, continues the movement. The very title (in German) defines the theme: the relation of divine justification to human justice. "Is there an actual, and therefore inward and vital, connection between the two realms? . . . Is there, in spite of all differences, an inner and vital connection between . . . what we are accustomed to call 'Divine Service' in the worship of the Church as such, and another form of service, what may be described as a 'political' service of God, a service of God which, in general terms, would consist in the careful examination of all those problems which are raised by the existence of human justice, of law, or, rather, which would consist in the recognition, support, defence, and extension of this law—and all this not in spite of, but because of, divine justification?"[78] Barth now discovers such an "inward and vital connection," and (as we have seen) tries to establish it through a Christological doctrine of the state that operates in terms of analogy and correspondence. However we may evaluate this theory, it is clear that Barth is now theologizing with direct and conscious political reference—aiming to call into question the legitimacy of the Hitler

[77] Barth, *op. cit.;* see below, p. 91.
[78] Barth, *Church and State,* pp. 9, 2; see below, pp. 106, 101–2.

state, which must be regarded as not really a state at all, but an "un-state."

The indictment of Nazi totalitarianism is vigorous and thoroughgoing. For the Christian, the chief criterion of the "lawful" state is whether it "grants legal protection to the free preaching of justification,"[79] not because the Church is thinking only of itself, but precisely because it is thinking of the world. The freedom of the Church is the guarantee of all freedom. "This right of the Church to liberty means the foundation, the maintenance, the restoration of everything—certainly of all human law. . . . All that can be said from the standpoint of divine justification on the question (and the questions) of human law is summed up in one statement: *the Church must have freedom to proclaim divine justification.*"[80] But this is precisely what the National-Socialist state refuses to grant. It denies the freedom of the Church not merely by its interference and attempts at "co-ordination," but above all by making upon its citizens an "*inward* claim," demanding of them not merely external obedience but the adoption of "a particular philosophy of life (*Weltanschauung*), or at least sentiments and reactions dominated by a particular view imposed by the state from without."[81] This is a religious demand, and "according to the New Testament, the only answer to this [kind of demand] is an unhesitating 'No!'."[82] Of course, persecution will come, but "the Church prefers to suffer persecution at the hands of the state which has become a 'beast out of the pit of the abyss,' rather than take part in the deification of Caesar. . . . Yet it still knows that it is responsible for the state and for Caesar, and it finally manifests this responsibility, 'the prophetic service of the Church as Watchman,' in its highest form, by praying for the state and for its offi-

[79] Barth, *op. cit.*, p. 65 (see also pp. 67, 68, 71, 73); see below, p. 137.
[80] Barth, *op. cit.*, pp. 84, 83; see below, p. 147.
[81] Barth, *op. cit.*, pp. 76–77; see below, p. 143.
[82] Barth, *op. cit.*, p. 77; see below, p. 143.

cials in all circumstances."[83] But praying for the "unjust"
state and its officials does not mean passive obedience. On
the contrary: "Can serious prayer, in the long run, continue
without the corresponding work? . . . Can we pray that
the state shall preserve us . . . without, in certain cases,
like Zwingli, reckoning with the possibility of revolution, the
possibility, according to his strong expression, that we may
have to 'overthrow with God' those rulers who do not follow
the line laid down by Christ?"[84]

Here we have, at last, in 1938, a fundamental statement
on the totalitarian state, which condemns it not merely because it does many wrong and evil things, but because by its
self-divinizing pretensions, demanding total allegiance to itself as the embodiment of a "particular philosophy of life,"
it is no longer the "lawful" state envisaged in Romans 13,
but the "beast out of the abyss" of Revelation 13. Here we
have at last a fundamental statement on the responsibility
of the Christian which envisages the possibility of revolution and war against the state which has become the "beast"
by becoming totalitarian.

In this work, too, Barth at last speaks out explicitly about
the necessity and possibility of making discriminate judgments in politics, where everything after all is bound to be
relative. No actual state can be either simply divine or simply diabolical, yet "there is clearly no cause for the Church
to act as though it lived, in relation to the state, in a night
in which all cats are gray. It is much more a question of continual decisions, and therefore of distinctions between one
state and another, between the state of yesterday and the
state of today."[85] Such discriminate judgment will bring
the Christian to the side of constitutional democracy.
"When I consider the deepest and most central content of
the New Testament exhortation," Barth declares, "I should
say that we are justified, from the point of view of exegesis,

[83] Barth, *op. cit.*, p. 11; see below, p. 107.
[84] Barth, *op. cit.*, pp. 79–80; see below, p. 145.
[85] Barth, *op. cit.*, pp. 31–32; see below, pp. 119–20.

45

in regarding the 'democratic conception of the state' as a justifiable expansion of the thought of the New Testament."[86] This "democratic conception of the state" Barth counterposes to "Fascism and Bolshevism alike," which he sees as "dethroned" wherever the "right of the Church to liberty" is recognized.[87] "The assertion that all forms of government are equally compatible or incompatible with the Gospel," he declares vehemently, "is not only outworn but false. It is true that a man may go to hell in a democracy, and achieve salvation under a mobocracy or a dictatorship. But it is not true that a Christian can endorse, desire, or seek after a mobocracy or a dictatorship as readily as a democracy."[88] No more forthright statement could be desired.

Another work of 1938, an address delivered in December of that year under the title of "The Church and the Political Question of Today," elaborates the new understanding of Nazi totalitarianism and the responsibility of the Church in eight brilliantly argued theses. National-Socialism is not merely a political regime; it is basically an "anti-Christian counter-church."[89] "This form of the state, total dictatorship in principle, confronts us with the question of God, and therefore becomes a question of faith."[90] "Between the witness of Jesus Christ and the domination of National-Socialism, there can be no peace";[91] Nazism may indeed be a "judgment of God upon the world and upon the Church," but that does not mean that we must stand helpless before it.[92] Islam, too, was a judgment of God, yet the Christian world rose against it in prayer and in struggle. "We, all Europe, and the entire Christian Church in Europe, are again

86 Barth, *op. cit.*, p. 80; see below, p. 145.
87 Barth, *op. cit.*, p. 84; see below, pp. 147–48.
88 Barth, *op. cit.*, p. 90, note 14; see below, p. 144, note.
89 Barth, "Die Kirche und die politische Frage von heute," in *Eine Schweizer Stimme, 1938–1945*, p. 87.
90 Barth, *op. cit.*, p. 84.
91 Barth, *op. cit.*, p. 94.
92 Barth, *op. cit.*, pp. 95–96.

confronted with a 'Turkish peril'; this time the 'Turks' have already taken Vienna and half of Prague."[93] Today, the regular Sunday prayer for the "National-Socialist state authority" has "become a problem."[94] Today, "Christians in Germany and the whole world should, in all seriousness, offer up the prayer included in the old Basel liturgy until the nineteenth century: 'Destroy the ramparts of the false prophet, Mohammed!' "[95]

Some months before, in September 1938, Barth had written to Joseph L. Hromadka in Prague, declaring emphatically that should Czechoslovakian soldiers take up arms against Nazi aggression, they would, in his view, be fighting for Christ and his Church.[96]

Actual war broke out next year, and in December 1939, Barth was writing to a French pastor, the editor of *Foi et Vie*,[97] explaining the special character of the war, pointing out the menace of Hitler's National-Socialism to the Church and to all of Europe and sharply criticizing the "eschatological defeatism . . . which, appealing to the truth that 'the whole world lieth in the evil one,' busies itself almost cynically with asserting that Hitler's present adversaries, for their part, are no saints either."[98] The democratic states are not, of course, "God's own warriors" (here one detects a qualification of the assurance given in the letter to Hromadka), but the Church "ought to say to them that we are privileged to be human and that we must defend ourselves with the power of desperation against the inbreaking of open inhumanity."[99] An easy victory is not to be expected

[93] Barth, *op. cit.*, p. 97.
[94] Barth, *op. cit.*, p. 96.
[95] Barth, *op. cit.*, p. 96.
[96] Barth, "Brief an Prof. Hromadka in Prag" (September 19, 1938), in *Eine Schweizer Stimme, 1938–1945*, pp. 58–59.
[97] Barth, *This Christian Cause* (Macmillan, 1941).
[98] Barth, "First Letter to the French Protestants" (December 1939), in *This Christian Cause* (the pages are not numbered, but this passage will be found on the sixth page of this Letter).
[99] Barth, *op. cit.*, fifth page of this Letter.

—there are "miracles of the antichrist"[100]—but the resolution of the Church and the people must not fail.

Just about a year later, after the fall of France, Barth wrote another letter to the French Protestants. The urgency of his appeal is greater than ever. "It is true, is it not," he demands, "that the armistice concluded between France and Germany has not altered in any respect the fact that you too are still, and even more now, involved in the conflict which is the root cause of the war, and in the responsibility for the existence of the conflict and for its solution?"[101] And he goes on: "We count on you that, as Christians and as Frenchmen, you will not leave us in the lurch, but will stand with us on the same side of the abyss —stand with us both inwardly, with your faith and prayers, and, as a result of this, also outwardly, with your words and deeds. . . ."[102] "Humility is an excellent thing," he grants; "let us only be sure, however, that if we preach about humility, it is a humility before God of which we are speaking, and not a humility before facts and circumstances, before Powers and Dominions, before men and human authorities."[103] The Church has not concluded an armistice with Hitler; "in the Church in France, the spiritual war must still go on."[104]

It is in this letter that Barth formulated his indictment of National-Socialism so much quoted in subsequent years. "National-Socialism," he thunders, "with its lies and cruelties, with its arbitrary justice, with its persecution of the Jews and its concentration camps, with its attacks upon, and poisoning of, the Christian Church, with its fundamental denial of freedom of, and consequently of responsibility for, thought and speech, with its conscious and

100 Barth, op. cit., tenth page of this Letter.
101 Barth, "Second Letter to the French Protestants" (October 1940), in This Christian Cause, second page of this Letter.
102 Barth, op. cit., second page of this Letter.
103 Barth, op. cit., eighth page of this Letter.
104 Barth, op. cit., tenth page of this Letter.

wicked repudiation of spiritual values—Nationalism-Social-
ism . . . has not changed. . . ."[105]

A much more extensive epistle Barth addressed to "his
dear Christian brethren in Great Britain" in April 1941. He
praises their resolution, but deplores their reliance on natural law as a really sure foundation for their resistance to
Hitler. "All arguments based on natural law," he insists, "are
Janus-headed. They do not lead to the light of clear decisions, but to the misty twilight in which all cats become
gray. They lead to—Munich."[106] Against natural law, he
urges his Christological foundation for political action. "Together we hear the word of Jesus Christ: 'All power is given
unto me in heaven and in earth'. . . . Taking our stand on
the truth of this word, you and I look at the events and
personalities of our time, and desire in the face of these
events and personalities, to take due account of our respon-
sibilities. Because this word is true, you desire, in the midst
of the storm and tumult of this war, to be and remain good
Britons, and you will do so; likewise, I desire to be and to
remain a good Swiss, and with God's help I will do so.
Everything which we today are seeking to defend, although
it may be in different places and in different ways, stands
or falls with the truth of this word."[107] The threat we are
confronted with is the "attempt of Adolf Hitler to force his
'New Order' on Central Europe today, on the whole of Europe tomorrow, and on the world the day after tomorrow.
The essence of this 'New Order' is the assertion of the
sovereignty of the German race and state, which in practice
is that of the German 'Führer' . . . impelled by the force
of a heathenish religion of blood, despotism, and war."[108]
What we are engaged in now is a "large-scale police measure, which has become absolutely necessary in order to re-

[105] Barth, op. cit., fourth and fifth pages of this Letter.
[106] Barth, "A Letter to Great Britain from Switzerland." In
This Christian Cause, seventeenth page of this Letter.
[107] Barth, op. cit., third page of this Letter.
[108] Barth, op. cit., sixth page of this Letter.

pulse an active anarchism which has become a principle.
. . . This is the only kind of war which we may be commanded to wage. Any other kind would be an encroach-
ment on the sovereign rights of God."[109] In this kind of
war, we need not despair, come what may. "We should
be slighting the resurrection of Jesus Christ, and denying
his reign on the right hand of the Father, if we forgot that
the world in which we live is already consecrated, and if
we did not, for Christ's sake, come to grips resolutely with
these spirits [the 'principalities and powers']. . . . It is only
as shadows without real substance that they can still beset
us. . . . The enterprise of Adolf Hitler, with all its clatter
and fireworks, and all its cunning and dynamic energy, is
the enterprise of an evil spirit, which is apparently allowed
its freedom for a time in order to test our faith in the resurrection of Jesus Christ, and above all to test our obedience
to that faith."[110]

The last of Barth's great wartime letters we are to examine is his "Letter to American Christians," written in December 1942.[111] This letter sets out to answer certain questions Barth had received from some American friends. Of
the seven questions put to him, he replies to only four. (It
is to be regretted that he did not find it possible to comment
on the fourth question: "What policy should the American
churches support with reference to relations (a) with Germany, (b) with Russia, after the war?") The war Barth
recognizes as a "particularly visible form of the judgment
of God upon mankind."[112] "Over against this judgment of
God, there are no degrees of guilt"; yet it cannot be denied
that "*this* group of nations (the United Nations today) has
on the whole remained more righteous than *that* one (the

109 Barth, *op. cit.*, twenty-first page of this Letter.
110 Barth, *op. cit.*, eleventh page of this Letter.
111 Barth, "A Letter to American Christians," *Christendom*,
Vol. VIII (1943), pp. 441–58. Comments on this letter by
American churchmen follow on pp. 458–72.
112 Barth, *op. cit.*, p. 443.

Axis coalition)."[113] This war is like a police action, and like a police action, it is at once a judgment of God, and a "dreadful ultimate instrument for the restoration of public order, broken and destroyed by mutual guilt."[114] "The fact that there is in war an 'enemy'—today his name is Hitler, and alas, also Germany—means simply that the disease from which we all suffered broke out in that spot and can only be cured by an operation in that place."[115] "The more readily we realize and admit that we all stand equally under God's judgment in this war, that this war in itself can assume the character of a serious 'police action,' which, while bringing unavoidable suffering over all, may be a defense of the 'righteous' state, and the less that we (who are in similar need of God's forgiveness) concentrate the war effort on any single guilty person or nation, the more cold-bloodedly and energetically will the war be waged, for then, and only then, will we have a good conscience in this hard and terrible business. As a serious, orderly police action, with the sober objective of destroying Hitler and rendering Germany and its allies harmless for all time to come, the war is in itself a beneficent and, despite all its harshness and terror, a merciful thing, which is in the truest interest of even those most directly hit thereby."[116] The Church ought to support the war effort, and so ought all Christians. "If the Church is really preaching the Word of God, then this will mean active support of the war effort insofar as it will testify, with a clarity consistent with the Word of God, that the carrying through of this stern police action against Hitler's nihilism is a necessary task of the righteous state; that therefore the U.S.A. has rightly embarked upon this task, and that the American Christian is obligated to help his country, within the framework of his vocation and his

[113] Barth, *op. cit.*, p. 443.
[114] Barth, *op. cit.*, p. 444.
[115] Barth, *op. cit.*, p. 444.
[116] Barth, *op. cit.*, pp. 445–46.

abilities, in the accomplishment of this task."[117] Barth criticizes American Christians for saying that they "abhor war," while at the same time they admit that "upon the outcome of this war depends the realization of Christian principles to which no Christian can be indifferent." "If the realization of Christian principles depends upon the outcome of this war," Barth insists, "then there is no point in the assurance that war is abhorrent, for it is surely only unnecessary and unjust wars that are condemned as abhorrent, and in this number the present one is not to be counted. If, conversely, war as such is really condemned, then the realization of Christian principles must definitely not be made dependent upon its outcome; that would mean the determination to do evil in violation of conscience in order that good may result."[118] The Church need not, in its preaching, repeat the exhortations and appeals of the state; that is already being sufficiently well done by other agencies. What then shall the Church preach in regard to the war? "The word of the reconciliation of the world with God through Jesus Christ . . . and nothing else. But this in its full scope! When [the Church preaches] about the sole sovereignty of Jesus Christ . . . [it is] actually preaching, through a simple, strict interpretation of the Biblical texts (and, as a rule, without naming persons and things specifically) against Hitler, Mussolini, and Japan; against anti-Semitism, idolization of the state, oppressive and intimidating methods, militarism, against all the lies and injustice of National-Socialism and Fascism in its European and its Asiatic forms, and thus [it] will naturally (and without 'dragging politics into the pulpit') speak on behalf of the righteous state and also for an honestly determined conduct of the war."[119]

"Identification of the Church with a political cause? No! Under no circumstances, and not even within the most mod-

[117] Barth, *op. cit.*, p. 447.
[118] Barth, *op. cit.*, p. 447.
[119] Barth, *op. cit.*, p. 448.

est limits!"[120] But "today's world-rending struggle . . . is being fought (whether mankind realizes and admits it or not) for his [Christ's] sake, and in honor of him. . . . Woe betide if the Church should desecrate itself in this cause instead of seeing to it, on the contrary, that this cause be consecrated through the Church."[121] Is the Church then "at war"? No, in the sense that the Church cannot become "one of the instruments of the warring state." Yes, in part at least, in the sense that the Church cannot be "neutral"; it cannot simply "look on and take care not to compromise itself." No again, and emphatically no, in the sense that "the Church in wartime lives and works—to the very degree that it takes the war seriously—in the deepest peace of the knowledge that he who makes all things new is already seated victoriously at the right hand of God."[122]

To Barth this conviction brings a sense of tranquility and assurance which makes him wonder at his American friends so busily concerned over "concrete plans" for the postwar world. "I cannot," he confesses, "get over the disproportion between these worries for the future and the present realities. . . . What is to be gained from drawing up these imaginative concepts in the form of a miniature eschatology? . . . Are you not the least bit disturbed over the trivial realization that obviously it is necessary, *now, now, now*, to act, help, fight with might and main, because the future may depend upon what is done now . . . or not done?"[123]

I have quoted at such length from Barth's wartime writings because it is in these writings, I am convinced, that Barth is to be seen at his best as a Christian interpreter of the great historical crisis of our time. Of course, there are many things that strike us as strange and perplexing in his conclusions, exhortations, and advice. Particularly disturb-

[120] Barth, *op. cit.*, p. 449.
[121] Barth, *op. cit.*, p. 450.
[122] Barth, *op. cit.*, p. 451.
[123] Barth, *op. cit.*, p. 452.

ing are the passages in which he seems to be operating with a too simple and unqualified contrast between "our" righteousness and "their" unrighteousness, without a sufficient realization of the ambiguity of even the best cause.[124] Nor can we feel very comfortable with Barth's insistence that if a war is necessary, it cannot be abhorrent; how can war ever be anything but abhorrent, all the more abhorrent when we have no recourse but to wage it?[125] We cannot overlook these points, and others that might be mentioned. Yet no one who has read Barth's writings from the mid-thirties to the early forties can deny the depth and power of his thought, his profound Christian insight, as revealed, for example, in his assessment of Nazism as an "anti-Christian counter-church," and his acute sense of the responsibility of the Church in the face of the totalitarian challenge. Despite all occasional excesses in one direction or the other,[126] his analysis is as balanced as it is penetrating, and his exhortations as sober in their realism as they are passionate in their conviction. We need not agree with his particular way of understanding politics and war in a Christian perspective to recognize in his political theologizing during these stormy

[124] Barth's letter to Joseph Hromadka (see above, p. 47) may be recalled as an example. Another example: "As far as Adolf Hitler is concerned, what we have to do is simply and solely to defend the Right against the Wrong. . . ." (Barth, "A Letter to Great Britain from Switzerland," in *This Christian Cause,* eighth page of this Letter.)

[125] This is one of John C. Bennett's criticisms of Barth's American Letter. Bennett writes: "A second criticism of Barth's statement is that he refuses to admit that while war is necessary it may still be abhorrent. . . . He makes the absurd claim that it is 'only unnecessary and unjust wars which are condemned as abhorrent. . . .' Mass slaughter, food blockades, and bombing of great cities, are still evil even though they may be necessary" ("Comment by John C. Bennett," *Christendom,* Vol. VIII [1943], p. 462).

[126] As far back as 1938, Reinhold Niebuhr was criticizing Barth for his readiness to identify his relative political judgments with the unconditional demands of faith (editorial, *Radical Religion,* Vol. IV [1938], pp. 4–5).

years the thinking of a great Christian theologian who has learned to take politics and culture with the utmost seriousness without for a moment abandoning his ultimate standpoint of faith, which infinitely transcends all political and cultural structures. Although Barth, in these years, always spoke within and out of particular historical situations, his thinking possesses an enduring significance, as relevant today as it ever was.

IV. BARTH'S ENCOUNTER WITH COMMUNISM

Unfortunately, the same cannot be said about Barth's encounter with Communism in the postwar years. It seems an altogether different Barth who is speaking, a Barth who has forgotten everything he had learned and taught the previous fifteen years.

It would be only too easy to present a detailed comparison of Barth's pronouncements in the two situations, exposing the glaring contradictions and inconsistencies in which he has involved himself, and perhaps something of the sort may prove necessary. But it is more important to try to understand what Barth is now saying, and to assess the implications of his new position.

It is obviously untrue to say that Barth is, in any sense, a supporter of Communist totalitarianism; he has made many statements which, at least on the face of it, repudiate the Communist "way of life" as not conforming to "our standards of justice and freedom," and brand totalitarianism a "dreadful thing."[127] But there is a certain detachment in his statements on Soviet despotism, and a curious

[127] "Are we not all convinced . . . that we cannot consider the way of life of the people in Soviet territory and in the Soviet-controlled 'People's democracies' to be worthy, acceptable, or of advantage to us, because it does not conform to our standards of justice and freedom?" (Barth, "The Christian Community in the Midst of Political Change" [1948], in *Against the Stream*, p. 116). "It has rightly been said that 'totalitarianism' is a dreadful thing" (Barth, *op. cit.*, p. 117).

ironic ring in his judgments. Above all, he refuses to do anything to arouse the Church to this new peril to human freedom and to the "lawful" democratic state, which only yesterday he was calling upon Christendom to defend to the last ditch. Everything he once said in denunciation of National-Socialism could be matched with easily available facts about Soviet totalitarianism, yet he keeps silent. The man who once wrote in the white heat of passion to Hromadka that the Czechoslovakian soldier who rose against the Nazi invaders would be fighting for Christ and his Church has nothing, absolutely nothing, to say about Soviet domination of East Europe and the ruthless suppression of the Hungarian revolution in 1956. Indeed, he condones, if he does not actually approve of, Hromadka's present participation in the Czechoslovakian Communist regime. The man who once saw in the totalitarian "form of the state" a challenge to the Christian faith is now unable to speak of Soviet totalitarianism without enclosing the word in quotation marks. The man who once bitterly excoriated the Church for having "no heart for millions unjustly persecuted" and for speaking, "if she speaks at all, only of her own affairs,"[128] is now advising the Church in Soviet-dominated countries to do precisely that. The man who once saw the "democratic conception of the state" as a "justifiable expansion of the thought of the New Testament" and defended the democratic state against "Fascism and Bolshevism alike,"[129] ridiculing those who were unable to make this all-important political distinction as men living in a "night in which all cats are gray,"[130] now urges a

[128] See Barth's letter to a German pastor, in Fritz Lieb, *Christ und Antichrist im Dritten Reich*, quoted by Gill, *Recent Protestant Political Theory*, pp. 95–96.

[129] Barth, *Church and State*, pp. 80, 84; see below, pp. 145, 147. "[The Church] will certainly withdraw from and oppose any out-and-out dictatorship such as the totalitarian state" (Barth, *Christian Community and Civil Community*, p. 37; see below, p. 174.

[130] Barth, *Church and State*, pp. 31–32; see below, p. 119.

"neutralism" which he himself only yesterday found so despicable. The man who was once so ready to speak up in indignation against every injustice and outrage is now too busy with his theological work to comment on the heroic effort of the Hungarian workers and intellectuals to throw off the yoke of Soviet tyranny.[131] In a word, the man who once aroused the Church to action now urges it to turn away from political involvement and remain indifferent to political actualities.

For that is precisely what Barth is urging today. "I am of the opinion," he says, "that the Church today, contrary to its action between 1933 and 1945, ought to stand quietly aloof from the present conflict and not let off all its guns before it is necessary, but wait calmly to see whether and in what sense the situation will grow serious again and call for speech."[132] How is it possible to understand this strange piece of advice coming from Barth?

Barth himself attempts to explain his position in his reply to Emil Brunner's open letter.[133] He repudiates the notion that the Church can act according to "principles." "The Church," he insists, "never thinks, speaks, or acts 'on principle.' Rather it judges spiritually and by individual cases. . . . It preserves the freedom to judge each new event afresh. If yesterday it travelled along one path, it is not bound to keep to the same truth today."[134] Why was it necessary for the Church to rouse itself and speak up

---

[131] See the letter of Barth's seminar in Basel defending him against Reinhold Niebuhr's criticism, "Barth on Hungary: An Exchange," *The Christian Century,* April 10, 1957.

[132] Barth, "The Christian Community in the Midst of Political Change," in *Against the Stream,* p. 117. This advice is repeated in various forms in Barth's writings to, or about, the Church in the Communist-dominated countries contained in *Against the Stream.*

[133] Brunner's letter and Barth's reply constitute Section 7 of "The Christian Community in the Midst of Political Change," in *Against the Stream,* pp. 106–18.

[134] Barth, *op. cit.,* p. 114.

against Nazism? Barth asks. A d he answers: because Hitler
and Hitlerism were an insidious temptation to the peoples
of Europe, and even to the Church, and so the Church had
to speak up. "The Central and Western European peoples
—first Germany, then the others—had succumbed to Hitler's
spell. He had become a spiritual, and almost everywhere, a
political source of temptation. . . . It was at that time that
I made my various attempts to make the Church ready for
action against the temptations of National-Socialism. . . .
At that t'ne, it had to warn men against tempters, to recall
those who had strayed, to rouse the careless, to 'confirm
the feeble knees,' to comfort sorrowing hearts."[135]

Today, however, the situation is altogether different.
Communism is no temptation to anyone in Europe today.
"In the last few years," Barth states in his reply to Brunner,
"I have become acquainted with western Germany, and
also with the non-Russian sectors of Berlin. Fear, distrust,
and hatred for the 'Eastern monster,' as you call it, I met
there in abundance, but apart from the German Communists, I met no man of whom I received the impression (as
one did with almost everybody in 1933) that he felt this
'monster' was a vexation, a temptation, an enticement, or
that he was in danger of liking it, or of condoning its deeds,
or of co-operating with it."[136] Everybody is against Communism, Barth says; therefore it is not necessary for the
Church to speak out. "I cannot admit that it is the duty of
Christians or of the Church to give theological backing to
what every citizen can, with much shaking of the head,
read in his daily paper and what is so admirably expressed
by Mr. Truman and by the Pope."[137] Today, the Church
"certainly has no cause to move against the stream and
thus to witness to Communism because it [Communism]
could never be worthy of it, either in its Marxist or its im-
perialist, let us say in its Asiatic, aspects. Must the Church

[135] Barth, *op. cit.*, pp. 114–15.
[136] Barth, *op. cit.*, p. 116.
[137] Barth, *op. cit.*, p. 116.

then move with the stream, and thus side with America and the Vatican? . . ."[138] No, Barth concludes; the situation today is not a repetition of the situation in the years 1933–45, and the tasks of the Church are different. Today, it is the task of the Church to "stand quietly aloof" and tread the "narrow path midway between Moscow and Rome."[139]

This is Barth's explanation—or rather, justification—of the line he is taking. We cannot deny that there is some force to his argument, although he surely ought to ask himself whether Communism is not in fact a serious "temptation" to some of his theological friends in Czechoslovakia, Hungary, and East Germany, who are inclined to see in Communist totalitarianism the "wave of the future" to which the Church must try to accommodate itself.[140] But most of all, Barth ought to ask himself whether he is being true to his own best insights developed in those Hitler years. Is it not obvious, from the record, that Barth's crusade against National-Socialism was based on far broader ground than

[138] Barth, *op. cit.*, pp. 116–17.
[139] Barth, *op. cit.*, pp. 117, 118.
[140] This is a point Brunner very justly makes against Hromadka in his open letter to Barth (Emil Brunner, "An Open Letter to Karl Barth," in *Against the Stream*, p. 111), and by Roger L. Shinn against Pastor Johannes Hamel in his review of Karl Barth and Johannes Hamel, *How to Serve God in a Marxist Land* (Association Press, 1959), appearing in *Worldview*, Vol. 2 (1959), p. 10. Brunner writes: "Your [Barth's] friend Hromadka defends the strange view that Communism—meaning the totalitarian Communism which is the only variety we are concerned with today—is an historical necessity, since democracy has proved its inability to survive; therefore, the Christian Church must welcome Communism." Shinn writes: "When Hamel extends his immediate testimony into broader theories of history and politics, he is on shakier ground. He comes dangerously close to the notion of the 'wave of the future,' which accepts any powerful historical movement as somehow God's work, which should not be opposed or reshaped." See also Gill (*Recent Protestant Political Theology*, p. 113) on "the 'wave of the future' theology of necessity put forward by Dr. Hromadka."

he is now willing to admit? Especially after 1938, his appeal came forth in the name of the Church's responsibility for mankind, for the "millions unjustly persecuted," for "public legality" and the "lawful state." Are not millions being unjustly persecuted today under Soviet totalitarianism? Are not "public legality" and the "lawful state" being endangered, if not altogether destroyed, by a regime that is nothing if not a "total dictatorship in principle"? The Church in western Europe would indeed be going "with the stream" by denouncing Communist totalitarianism, but was this not what Barth was asking his English and American friends to do when he wrote to them his letters of 1941 and 1942? Barth refuses to urge the Church to speak out against Communist totalitarianism because are not the " 'Christian' peoples of the West [and] the Americans . . . already sure enough of the justice of their cause against Russia without this truth ['that "totalitarianism" is a dreadful thing'], and our Christian support"?[141] But were not the English in 1941 and the Americans in 1942 equally sure of the justice of their cause and of the evils of totalitarianism, yet Barth thought it most necessary to instruct them and strengthen their resolution. Barth feels that the Church in the West would be in a false position if it tried to exhort the "poor Russians and even the poor Communists" against totalitarianism, because the "Western Church in the old days and even today has [itself] accepted so much totalitarianism. . . ."[142] But was it not Barth who, back in December

[141] Barth, "The Christian Community in the Midst of Political Change," in *Against the Stream*, p. 117.

[142] Barth, *op. cit.*, p. 117. Barth also denies the Western democracies the right to condemn Soviet Communism because they "have not yet tackled anything like energetically enough . . . the social problem," which, according to Barth, "has been tackled in Soviet Russia, albeit with very dirty and bloody hands and in a way that rightly shocks us" (*op. cit.*, p. 139). He is apparently unable to see that while "the capitalism of the West may have corrupted but did not destroy democracy . . . the 'socialism' of Communism did produce absolute despotism"

1940, warned the French Protestants against an "eschatological defeatism . . . which busies itself almost cynically
with asserting that Hitler's present adversaries, for their
part, are no saints either"?[143]

Barth is not content with pointing up what he takes to be
a fundamental difference between the earlier and the later
situation. He attempts to make certain positive distinctions
which would put Communism in a more favorable light.
"In sharp contrast to his attitude toward Nazism," Charles
West notes, "he [Barth] finds Communism at least a system which has made a serious attempt to solve the social
problem."[144] Moreover, Barth insists, "Communism, as distinguished from Nazism, has not done, and by its nature
cannot do, one thing: it has never made the slightest attempt to reinterpret or falsify Christianity, or to shroud itself in a Christian garment . . . and it has never committed
the crime of anti-Semitism."[145] How seriously are we to
take these arguments? The "social achievements" of the
National-Socialist revolution were also the great pride of
Nazi propaganda (as Emil Brunner has pointed out),[146]
and Barth's Social-Democratic friends would surely have
much to tell him about the quality and character of Communism's efforts to "solve the social problem" under totalitarianism.[147] As to Communism not attempting to "rein-

(Reinhold Niebuhr, "Why Is Barth Silent on Hungary?", *The
Christian Century,* January 23, 1957).

[143] Barth, "First Letter to the French Protestants," in *This
Christian Cause,* sixth page of this Letter.

[144] West, *Communism and the Theologians,* p. 300; see
Barth, "The Church Between East and West," in *Against the
Stream,* p. 139.

[145] Barth, "The Christian Community in the Midst of Political
Change," in *Against the Stream,* p. 140.

[146] Brunner, "An Open Letter to Karl Barth," in *Against the
Stream,* pp. 110–11.

[147] "If I am correctly informed," Brunner writes in his open
letter to Barth, "you are still a Socialist. . . . Socialism is engaged in a life and death struggle against Communism because
and insofar as it [Socialism] is fundamentally anti-totalitarian.

terpret or to falsify" Christianity, Barth forgets that his indictment against Nazism on this score was part of his larger
indictment of National-Socialism as a *Heilsanstalt* (redemp-
tive institution) and an "anti-Christian counter-church."[148]
Where, more clearly than in Communism, can we find a
political system claiming to be a *Heilsanstalt*, with a total
demand and a total *Weltanschauung*, thus in effect raising
itself as an "anti-Christian counter-church" in consummate
form? And anti-Semitism? It is enough to note that Barth
was writing his exculpatory words just about the time that
Stalin was launching his extermination campaign against
the Jews as "rootless cosmopolitans" and "homeless intellectuals"—the very same Stalin whom Barth lauds as a "man
of stature," not to be mentioned "in the same breath"
with such "charlatans as Hitler, Göring, Hess, Goeb-
bels. . . ."[149]

No; Barth's apologia will not do, and even his followers,
at least the more critical of them, admit it. Charles West,
in a most thoughtful and appreciative review of Barth's
thinking on Communism, finds Barth poorly informed about
Communism and guilty of "ineptitude . . . in the field of
social and political decision."[150] We could be well content
to leave it at that. Yet one cannot help wondering. What
is the reason for this strange change in Barth—or is it, as
some have suggested, really a reversion to the earlier Barth,
with whom churchly concern for politics had gone "underground for a period"?[151] How shall we account for his

---

Is it therefore a good thing that this anti-totalitarian Socialism
should be attacked in the rear—by churchmen of all people—
in the defensive fight against totalitarian Communism?" (Brunner, "An Open Letter to Karl Barth," *Against the Stream*, pp.
109–10).

[148] Barth, "Die Kirche und die politische Frage von heute," in
Eine Schweizer Stimme, pp. 80, 87.

[149] Barth, "The Church Between East and West," in *Against
the Stream*, p. 139.

[150] West, *Communism and the Theologians*, p. 304.

[151] West, *op. cit.*, p. 184.

blind prejudice against America which makes his "Letter to a Pastor in the German Democratic Republic"[152] such embarrassing reading—and this after he had, in 1942, castigated American churchmen for even raising the question of "American imperialism"?[153] How can one explain his refusal to see the reality of Soviet imperialism—especially after he had himself, in 1942, suggested the possibility of "all sorts of new and perhaps worse forms of imperialism" arising after the war, with specific mention of "Soviet Russia"?[154] And, finally, what can we make of Barth's sneering references, so frequent in his writings recently, to "Mr. Truman and the Pope," "America and the Vatican," "Moscow and Rome"?[155]

It is perhaps better not to inquire too closely into such matters; it would get nowhere. Let us be grateful to Barth for the great service he has rendered in deepening and illumining our theological understanding of social questions by his writings in the Hitler era; let us be grateful, too, for the elements of truth contained in his recent thinking, for we above all need to learn never to identify our cause, however just, with the cause of God. What Karl Barth has

[152] Barth, "Letter to a Pastor in the German Democratic Republic," in Karl Barth and Johannes Hamel, *How to Serve God in a Marxist Land.*

[153] Barth, "A Letter to American Christians," *Christendom,* Vol. VIII (1943), pp. 457–58.

[154] Barth, *op. cit.,* p. 457.

[155] Barth, "The Christian Community in the Midst of Political Change," in *Against the Stream,* pp. 116, 117, 118. Opposition to Communism Barth regards as yielding to the "temptation of following the lead of the Romans" (*op. cit.,* p. 104). West notes of Niemöller, Heinemann, and their friends that, "curiously enough, the crisis and confessional element of Barth's political teaching [here] reemerges. Not against Communism, but against Adenauer and his conception of the defence of a Christian Europe, the Christian is called to declare his binding 'No,' to point out the evil spirit at work, and even call the unity of the Church into question by its response to this political confession" (West, *Communism and the Theologians,* p. 303).

taught us about the state, about totalitarianism, and about our political responsibility in the perspective of faith we are not likely to forget. And even on Communism we may hope that Barth has not yet said his last word.[156]

V. CONCLUSION

Perhaps the best over-all estimate of Barth's teaching in the field with which we are concerned has been given by Charles West in his recent work, *Communism and the Theologians*. West finds three elements in Barth's thinking which are of central significance:

1. *Barth's conception of the state as an order of redemption in correspondence with the "heavenly polis."* "The basic structure of political life is, for Barth, the *Gegenüber* of the two *Bundesordnungen* (orders of the covenant) which belong to the sphere of redemption: Church and state, or, as Barth's more developed thinking names them, *Christengemeinde* and *Bürgergemeinde*."[157] In this view, "no political order [can be] justified by less than its service to the end of man's redemption, however external this service may be . . . [thus making] the Christian . . . a radical toward every political system and loyalty, more consistently radical than the Communist himself, and yet at the same time more positive, more constructive, than any idealist, in affirming and discovering the true service of the state."[158]

2. *Barth's conception of political activity as a "free, direct approach to human beings and their welfare."*[159] Every-

[156] Some encouragement may be derived from the rebuke which Barth administered in 1951 to the Hungarian Bishop Berecsky when the latter adopted an "attitude toward the Communistic government of Hungary which seemed almost to identify it with a second source of revelation. . . . [Barth] warned him of the similarity between his thinking and that of the 'German Christians' in Nazi times" (West, *op. cit.*, p. 322).

[157] West, *op. cit.*, p. 292.

[158] West, *op. cit.*, p. 305.

[159] West, *op. cit.*, p. 304.

where in Europe, West believes, "Barthian theology has contributed . . . toward breaking down ideological politics in favor of a more pragmatic and practical approach to problems of state."[160]

3. *Barth's emphasis on the "note of crisis and confession in politics."*[161] Political questions are not merely, or even primarily, technical questions of adjustment and accommodation; they are sometimes, especially in times of crisis, questions in which "spirits are tested," when what is demanded is an attitude that is not only politically responsible but also confessionally true.

Such, West believes, are the basic constitutive elements of Barth's political thinking, and with this opinion we may agree. We may also agree with West's further conclusion that "Barth . . . fails precisely in that synthesis of his three theological elements which would give his political judgment depth and validity. At different times, we find different aspects stressed. . . . [In one case or another] a different element of his theology predominates. In no case does he adequately relate them to produce a fully convincing political ethic. In one situation [Nazism], we are confronted with an unmodified declaration of crisis and *status confessionis* against the political demons of our day, and in another [Communism] we find counsel to wait, reserve judgment, and remember that God's grace rules even the demons. And we find this arbitrary selection from differ-

---

[160] West, *op. cit.*, p. 306. West points particularly to Holland and to Germany. "In Germany . . . the influence of the Confessing Church from the days of the Nazis has prevented the regrowth of a political party of Evangelical-Conservative background, such as was the old Deutsche Nationale Volkspartei, and has at the same time contributed to the unideological realism of the Christian Democratic Union, preventing it from becoming once again a Catholic party, and to reconciliation of the Evangelical Church with the Social Democrats" (*op. cit.*, p. 306, note 1). It may be added that Barth himself and many of his followers are violently opposed to the Christian Democrats.

[161] West, *op. cit.*, p. 306.

ent theological emphases for different political situations justified by appeal to Christian freedom in response to Christ!"[162]

Barth's failure to integrate his theology of politics, despite the profundity of his insights, makes the Christian realism of Reinhold Niebuhr particularly relevant, West thinks. "Niebuhr's concentration on the facts of human political experience, and his theology of continuing tension between love and law in political decision, compels him to take the realities of human social experience in all their complexity, which Barth's theology allows, to be sure, but does not compel. Niebuhr's doctrine of sin and grace operates in each political analysis and decision to produce greater political realism than Barth. He balances more accurately the demonic and the creative forces at work. He is more aware of the balance between relativity (and sin) and confessional urgency in concrete decisions. He is, in short, without falling into any pattern of natural law, more acutely aware than Barth of the ways of God with human structures of power, order, and justice, precisely because, or so it seems, of his refusal to place the whole political process from the beginning under the order of redemption. Barth seems, because of his doctrine of all-embracing grace, to neglect his responsibility for that difficult empirical analysis of real human relations, most especially in politics, which the Christian, just because of his faith, should take more seriously than all others. His movement from theology to political decision is forever beset by oversimplification of the political issues, and by blindness to some of the facts involved, not less when he speaks of freedom than when he speaks of crisis or of the structure of the just state."[163]

[162] West, *op. cit.*, pp. 312–13.

[163] West, *op. cit.*, pp. 313–14. It is interesting that West traces Niebuhr's creative realism to the fact that, unlike Barth, he refuses to "place the whole political process from beginning to end under the order of redemption." Many years before, Wilhelm Pauck, commenting on Barth's American Letter, had noted:

In these words, West puts his finger on Barth's weakness, but it is a weakness that comes out of strength. And that strength is immense, for it comes out of a depth-understanding of the Christian faith given to few in our time.

"I do not find Barth's doctrine of the 'righteous state' acceptable. . . . It is derived from his concept of revelation and thus placed upon too narrow a base. This opinion can be proved, it seems to me . . . by the fact that he cannot find a proper interpretation of the Soviet state (or does he, to some degree at least, regard Soviet Russia as a state that is righteous in his Christian theological sense?)" ("Comment by Wilhelm Pauck," *Christendom*, Vol. VIII [1943], p. 469).

COMMUNITY, STATE, AND CHURCH

GOSPEL AND LAW

I

If I chose the title, *"Law and Gospel,"* I would have to speak in terms of the formula which has come to be taken almost for granted among us. But I should like immediately to call attention to the fact that I shall not speak about "Law and Gospel" but about *"Gospel and Law."* The traditional order, "Law and Gospel," has a perfect right in its place, which we shall later describe. It must not, however, define the structure of the whole teaching to be outlined here. The nature of the case is such that anyone who really and earnestly would first say Law and only then, presupposing this, say Gospel would not, no matter how good his intention, be speaking of the Law of *God* and therefore then certainly not of *his* Gospel. This usual way is, even in the most favorable case, enveloped in ambiguities of every sort.

Anyone who wishes correctly to approach our subject must speak first of the *Gospel*. This makes us think immediately of that 430-year interval after which, according to Galatians 3:17, the Law followed the promise. It *must* follow the promise, but it must *follow* the promise. And while the Law follows the promise, the *fulfillment* of the promise follows it in turn, and this fulfillment, only this, contains the Law's own fulfillment. The Law would not be the Law if it were not hidden and enclosed in the ark of the *covenant*. And the Gospel, too, is only the Gospel if the Law—that which "came in between" (Romans 5:20)—is *hidden* and *enclosed* in it as in the ark of the covenant. The Gospel is not Law, just as the Law is not Gospel; but because the Law is in the Gospel, from the Gospel, and points to the Gospel, we must first of all know about the Gospel in order to know about the Law, and not vice versa.

We must, however, immediately clarify this: anyone who wishes correctly to approach our subject must speak first of the content of the Gospel, of God's *grace*. We agree on this (how could we justify a different statement in the face of Holy Scripture?): if we speak of Gospel *and* if we speak of Law, we mean God's Word. God's Word can indeed say many things to us. It not only can comfort us, heal us, vivify us, it not only can instruct and enlighten us, it can also judge us, punish us, kill us, and it actually does all of these. But let us not overlook three things:

1. The Word of God is the one "Word of truth," the Word of the "Father of light in whom is no variation or alternation of light and darkness" (James 1:17 f.). According to Scripture, the contrast of Gospel and Law certainly designates a duality. It can even designate a struggle. But their peace in the one Word of this Father is greater than their duality and their struggle.

2. The Word of God, when it is addressed to us and when we are allowed to hear it, demonstrates its unity in that it is always *grace;* i.e., it is free, non-obligatory, undeserved divine goodness, mercy, and condescension. A Gospel or a Law which we speak to ourselves, by virtue of our own ability and trusting in our own authority and credibility, would, as such, not be *God's* Word; it would not be *his* Gospel and it would not be *his* Law. The *very fact that* God speaks to us, that, under all circumstances, is, in itself, grace.

3. The Word of God preserves this its form by being also in its content, whatever it says, properly and ultimately *grace: free, sovereign* grace, *God's* grace, which therefore can also mean being Law, which also means judgment, death, and hell, but *grace* and nothing else. Every

72

apparently different content which we could ascribe to the
Word of God proves, considering the Old Testament pre-
dictive witness as well as the New Testament witness of fulfillment, to be included in this as relative to this content,
to God's grace. A word of God with a really different content would as such, in any case, not be a Word of the
triune God, whom Holy Scripture proclaims. If we hear this
Word of God, then we hear—grace. Precisely because the
Gospel has grace as its *particular direct* content, which then
also includes, in itself, the content of the Law, it enforces
its *priority* over the Law which still, included in the Gospel
and relative to it, is no less God's Word.

Thus it is above all necessary that we speak of this content of the Gospel. God's *grace,* which is this content—which
also includes the Law, if it really is *God's* Word and Law
—this grace is called, and is, *Jesus Christ.* For this is God's
grace, that the eternal Word of God *became flesh.* Flesh
means "like one of us." God's Word does not transform himself into flesh. How would it be grace if God ceased to be
God, even if he could? What kind of mercy would he show
us thereby? No, that the Word *became* flesh means that
without ceasing to be God, he added our humanity to and
assimilated it in his deity, in indissoluble but also unmixed
unity with himself; and let us be clear, this refers to our
humanity in the shape resulting from sin's darkening and
destruction. Therefore, this was done not for the sake of
the power or honor or any other attribute of humanity, but
because of the Word's own good pleasure, because of his
incomprehensible love and that which is the sign: "born of
the Virgin Mary." This is God's grace: our ordinary humanity is not the only humanity, but in Jesus Christ, God's own
humanity, the humanity of his Word, and in him, in this
his abasement to our lowliness, his divinity is present for
us others; we participate in his divinity, we are exalted to
him. And now this eternal Word of God, because he bore
flesh, has borne the need, the curse, the punishment which
stamps and characterizes man as flesh. This punishment is

God's answer to the sin of man. Sin consists in autocracy, but thus to absolutize the self is godlessness. That this is true becomes apparent in man's aversion and flight precisely from the grace of God. God's answer to sin—this is also grace—is our being as flesh: we must die. If we would *hear* this answer, this would be our *salvation*. We would then, considering that we must die (Psalms 90:12), in the knowledge of our lostness as the people that is grass (Isaiah 40:7), repent and, our autocracy destroyed, inherit eternal life. For one reason and one alone does God will the death of the godless: that he turn away from his nature and live (Ezekiel 18:21 f., and parallels). But who hears this answer? Who acknowledges it? Who bows before it? None of us! At this point, God's grace runs into our hatred of grace. But this is the proper work of grace, that his eternal Word —by his becoming flesh, by his remaining obedient in the flesh, by his suffering punishment and therefore dying, because of this obedience—undertook to give the saving answer in our place, to expose our human autocracy and godlessness, to confess man's lostness, to acknowledge the justice of God's judgment against us, and thus to accept the grace of God. This is what Jesus Christ did for us "during his whole lifetime on earth, but especially at its end" (answer to question 37 of the Heidelberg catechism). He quite simply *believed*. (πίστις Ἰησοῦ in Romans 3:22; Galatians 2:16, etc. should certainly be understood as a subjective genitive!) And in this faith, he bore our punishment—not first of all, for instance, to give us an example (he certainly also did that!), but first of all and above all representatively. This is God's grace: that our humanity is, insofar as it is ours, not only condemned and lost because of our sins (our perpetually new sins!) but at the same time, insofar as it is the humanity of Jesus Christ, it is justified by God and accepted *in* the judgment and *in* the lostness because Jesus Christ—only the eternal Word of God could do this —believed; i.e., he said not "no" but "yes" to grace and thus to man's state of being judged and lost. But this justification and acceptance of our humanity is really accomplished in the *resurrection* of Jesus Christ from the *dead*. God's eternal Word in his unity with the flesh is not only the promise but the fulfillment of the promise that man's repentance will be his salvation, that the just will *live* by his faith. Therefore, because he took the form of a servant and thus and therein was obedient unto death, God has exalted him (Philippians 2:6f.). Grace also triumphed and revealed itself as grace in him, the one and only person who allowed God's grace validity as grace in the flesh, because he was the eternal Word that became flesh. The one who accepted death as the wages of sin—and thus precisely preserved his sinlessness—this is the one whom death could not hold, the one whose life had to *devour* death, and *did*. And this is God's grace, that we can see as the end of all humanity, insofar as it is ours, certainly nothing else ahead of us except the infirmity of old age, the hospital, the battlefield, the cemetery, decay, or ashes; but to the extent that it is at the same time the humanity of Jesus Christ, just as definitely—no, much more definitely—nothing else ahead of us but resurrection and eternal life.

Consequently, God's grace, his grace for our humanity, the goodness, mercy, and condescension in which he is our God and as such accepts us, is Jesus Christ, he himself and he uniquely. He himself and he uniquely is therefore the content of the Gospel. Grace, and that means the content of the Gospel, consists therefore simply in the fact that Jesus Christ with his humanity, which he assumed in his birth, preserved as obedience in his death, glorified in his resurrection—he himself and he uniquely intercedes for us with our humanity. He *can* do it because he is not only like one of us but is God's son and thus himself God, the judge before whom he undertakes the responsibility for us. And he *does* it, because it is his unfathomable pleasure to make this use of his divine power, to utilize a love which expects no love in return and finds none, which encounters us only and always and in all cases as free and pure love. According to this, the state and course of the *man* under grace must be characterized as the state and course of one for whose humanity Jesus Christ *intercedes* with his assumed, obedient, and glorified humanity and does so because man himself and of himself has neither any willingness nor ability to believe. Jesus Christ intercedes completely so that thus man's own humanity, as Paul likes to put it, is dead, but is alive only because he is "in Christ," i.e., because Jesus Christ has become, grammatically speaking, his subject. "I have been crucified with Christ. I live, but no longer I, but Christ lives in me. For the life I now live in the flesh, I live in the faith of the Son of God" (this is to be understood quite literally: I live—not, for instance, somehow in my belief in the Son of God, but in the fact that the Son of God believed!), "who loved me and gave himself for me" (Galatians 2:20). The state and course of the man under grace is thus expressed in the Old Testament: "He who dwells in the shelter of the Highest, and abides in the shadow of the Almighty, says to the Lord: My refuge and my fortress, my God in whom I hope" (Psalms 91:1). That he is in the communion of the saints, that he has received the forgiveness of sins, that he is hastening toward the resurrection of the body and the life everlasting—these things this man believes, but they have no reality, they have not even a partial reality in his faith, in the triumph of his faith; they only have reality in the fact that the Lord Jesus Christ, who was born a man for us, died for us and rose for us, is also his Lord, his refuge, his fortress, his God. Jesus Christ, he himself and he alone is the grace bestowed upon such a man.

II

Now, in the second place, it is time to speak of the *Law*. We have said that just as the Gospel is not the Law, the Law is not the Gospel. We would contradict the whole of Holy Scripture if we were unwilling to distinguish between the two. But we could also not, according to what we have said, glance over from the Gospel to the Law as to a second entity next to and outside of the Gospel. We would, again, contradict the whole of Holy Scripture if we wished to separate the two here. If we wish to avoid both mistakes, we must now proceed from what Scripture indubitably attests concerning *Jesus Christ* (of whom we heard: he is grace, he is the content of the Gospel), i.e., that he has satisfied the Law, has fulfilled the Law, keeping it by obedience to its commands. In defining the Law, we shall in no case be permitted to break loose from this fact—that Jesus Christ, because he was the "evident grace of God" (Titus 2:11), at the same time kept the commands of the Law; instead, we shall have to begin with it. This fact will not only form the criterion by which we must measure all of our self-constructed concepts of Law and norm. It will also have to become the canon of interpretation of everything called Law in the Old Testament and New Testament: the deciding element, that which is really intended in every great or small, internal or external command, has to be understood from the fulfillment of each of them in Jesus Christ.

"The Law is the manifest will of God." The definition is correct. But where is the will of God manifest? Certainly God is the Creator of all things and thus Lord of all that occurs. He and his will, and thus the Law, are, however, not manifest to us in all things, in every occurrence, that is, so very manifest that our apprehensions of it could claim to be more and something different than our own theories and interpretations. If the Law is also *God's Word*, if it is further *grace* that God's Word is spoken aloud and becomes audible, and if grace means nothing else than *Jesus Christ*, then it is not only uncertain and dangerous but perverse to want to understand the Law of God on the basis of any other thing, of any other event which is different from the event in which the will of God, tearing in two the veil of our theories and interpretations, is visible as grace in both form and content. This event is, however, the occurrence of the will of God at Bethlehem, at Capernaum and

Tiberias, in Gethsemane, on Golgotha and in the garden of Joseph of Arimathea. Because this occurrence of the will of God, therefore the occurrence of his grace, becomes *manifest* to us, the *Law* becomes manifest to us. From what God does *for* us, we infer what he wants *with* us and *from* us. His grace does apply to *us*, it does concern us. Also, and precisely in his grace, he does demonstrate that he certainly acts for us and toward us, but for and toward *us* as his creatures in the relative but real differentiation of their existence and nature as creatures from his as Creator. His action does not revolve in itself; instead, it has its goal in our action, in the conformity of our action with his own. "You must"—more exactly and correctly, *"You shall"*—"be perfect, as your heavenly father is perfect" (Matthew 5:48). Grace can by no means become manifest to men unless it means this offense, unless it moves in this future tense: "You shall be!" Yes, the revelation of grace as such *is* this offense. Given the validity of this indicative, "that I am not my own but his, my faithful Saviour Jesus Christ's," then precisely this its validity establishes the *Ten Commandments*, together with its exposition in the *Sermon on the Mount*, and its application in the *apostolic instructions*. Grace needs only to become known among us. Whether it be originally in the faith of all the Biblical witnesses, as prophecy and expectation through the prophets, or as recollection and proclamation through the apostles, precisely its publication establishes the *Law*. The divine justification of universally sinful men by the faith of Jesus Christ is attested, according to Romans 3:21, by the *Law* and the *prophets*. The promulgation of the divine *commands* proclaims the grace promised in the covenant between God and Israel. But the significance of the New Testament apostolate, which always looks back on the accomplished fulfillment, is also the summons to the Church, and that means to the *obedience* of faith (Romans 1:5); then, therefore, the rejection of its message is decisively designated as disobedience (Romans 10:21; 11:30; 15:31).

78

And John the Baptist, as the preacher of *repentance*, stands, quite appropriately in the middle between Moses and Paul, pointing to the present Messiah. "You will be!" "All of you will be!" This, and thus God's Law, is what they all perceived in the revelation of the grace in which they participated—it makes no difference whether it meant future, present, or past to them—and transmitted as their witness to this revelation. But God's Law, an entirely definite, demanding, claiming, will of God also meets those who are in the Church—in the *Church,* concretely in its preaching, in its sacraments, in its confession. How could the Lordship of Jesus Christ be proclaimed, unless the proclamation as such be a demand for *obedience?* How the incarnation except as the command of self-denial? How the cross of Christ, except as the command to *follow after* him and take up one's own cross? How then his resurrection except as under the admonition of the Easter pericope of the ancient Church (I Corinthians 5:7 f.): *"Cleanse out the old leaven* that you may be new dough!"*? Precisely faith in the article concerning the standing and falling of the Church (*articulus stantis et cadentis ecclesiae*), in the message about the justification of the sinner through the reconciliation which took place in the blood of Christ, means *purification, sanctification, renewal,* or it means nothing at all; it is unfaith, false faith, superstition. "And by this we may be sure that we know him, if we keep his commandments. He who says, 'I know him' but disobeys his commandments is a liar, and the truth is not in him" (I John 2:3 f.). Yes, and further, the Church would not be the Church if, in her very existence, but also in her teaching and keeping of the Law of God, its *commands,* its *questions,* its *admonitions,* and its *accusations* would not become visible and apprehensible also for the world, for state and society—even if they do not receive precisely the message concerning the grace of the triune God, expressed in the three articles of faith, the message which uniquely constitutes the task of the Church. The Church would not be the Church if these aspects of the

Law would not, as such, become the prophetic witness *for* the will of God *against* all of men's sinful presumption, *against* all their lawlessness and unrighteousness. Thus, we can certainly make the general and comprehensive statement that the Law is nothing else than the necessary *form of the Gospel*, whose content is grace. Precisely this content demands this form, the form which calls for its like, the Law's form. If grace is manifest, if it is attested and proclaimed, it means demand and claim upon man. If there is faith in Jesus Christ, the one who is coming or has come, if his name is proclaimed, grace means the office of Moses and Elijah, of Isaiah and Jeremiah, the office of the Baptizer, of Paul, of James. Grace, by becoming the summons to grace, means the Church which dares and must dare to speak with authority.

In this way, then, the *Law is in the Gospel* as the tablets from Sinai were in the ark of the covenant, in such a way that the *Gospel* is always *in the Law* as that which is manifest, proclaimed, as that which concerns man in the crib and in swaddling clothes of the commands, of the command and order of God. Therefore, Paul quite seriously calls the Law holy and its commands holy, right, and good (Romans 7:12). Therefore, he denies that it is against the promises of God (Galatians 3:21). Therefore, he says that it rather promises us life (Romans 7:10). Therefore, he asserts (in agreement with the familiar words of the Sermon on the Mount in Matthew 5:16 f.) that the proclamation of faith means not the abrogation but the establishment of the Law (Romans 3:21). Therefore, he designates himself—and does so, let it be understood, precisely in his character as the apostle to the Gentiles—as one under the Law of Christ (ἔννομος Χριστοῦ, I Corinthians 9:21). Therefore, he can say in prosaic terms, and not at all hypothetically, that only the doers of the Law will be justified (Romans 2:13). Therefore, the praise of the Law, in the form in which it is peculiar to the message concerning Christ in the Old Testament, by no means ceases in that of the New Testament.

And why should it? The distinction between Gospel and Law has been compared with that between heaven and earth, or between day and night. The differentiation between content and form, however, also designates an infinite distinction. But what does this distinction mean? It certainly can *not* mean a distinction between more and less, better and worse, or even the distinction between divine and human or good and evil! The fact that there is an earth under the heavens, that day is day in its alternation with night, that the content of the Gospel also has a form, is not simply one more of God's works, but is precisely the work of God which makes room for the Gospel in our human sphere and room for us men in the sphere of the Gospel. In view of this work of God, how could praise be lacking, how could it ever cease? No, the praise of the Law of God, as it is sung for example in Psalm 119, will not grow old throughout all eternity. Although the Law is not the Gospel, without the Law, we would, in fact, not have the Gospel either.

When we come, however, to answer the question, "What does God in his Law want with us and from us?" we shall, unless we wish to go astray, have to come back again in all strictness to the *content* of the Gospel, to the fact that Jesus Christ has fulfilled the Law and kept all the commands. The Law does bear witness to the grace of God; in this way, it is the form of the Gospel, in this way it is claim and demand, call to repentance and prophecy. In testifying to God's grace, it says to us, "You should"—no, "You shall be!" However, God's grace is Jesus Christ, who intercedes for us with his humanity. He intercedes for us, however, by believing in our place—it took the eternal Word incarnate to do that—and that means by saying "yes" to God's glory and thus to man's misery. By this, his believing, he accomplished once for all what God wants with man and from him: he fulfilled the Law and kept all the commands. All the commands point to, they bear witness to this faith, which *he* alone demonstrated. And, therefore,

81

if the Gospel becomes manifest, this faith of Jesus Christ, which is the heart and star of the Gospel, becomes that form which requires conformity, and therefore the command in all commands, the principle of our cleansing, sanctification, and renewal, the One in all that the Church has to say both to itself and to the world. For if Jesus Christ has done *this* in our place, what then becomes of *us?* Men, beloved brothers, what should *we* do then? This question is laid before us and upon us with the entire dignity and gravity of the divine Law itself—and already before the question, its answer: You shall believe! You, you who have other gods beside me, you who make for yourselves pictures of me, who misuse my name, profane the Sabbath, are disobedient to father and mother, who kill, who commit adultery, who steal, who bear false witness against your neighbor, covet what belongs to him—you shall (and that will be the negation and reversal of everything) believe, *you shall* love and fear God, not in contradicting these your sins, not in struggling against them, but in completely and consistently eradicating them, for even the smallest sin would still be the whole, the deadly sin. And this will be your conformity with that form of the Gospel, your obedience, then, to God's law! It is true, therefore, that all commandments are included in the *first* commandment and always must be understood and explained as especially emphasizing the first commandment.

What then does precisely this first commandment mean, if we are not permitted to understand it as anything else than as the form of the Gospel? What does it mean to fear and to love God? What does it mean to believe? The faith of Jesus Christ, in which grace has occurred and at the same time the Law has been fulfilled, is a unique act which cannot be repeated. Once more, this occurrence required the eternal Word in flesh. Being certain Jesus Christ is God but we are men, we will do well not to try to imitate Jesus in this faith and thus to believe *as* Jesus believed. However, the meaning of the first commandment and thus of all the commandments, and thus of our obedience to God's Law, can and must be that we believe *in* Jesus Christ, that we— since the Word became flesh, remained obedient in the flesh, and was exalted in the flesh—acknowledge his representative faith, which we will never realize, and allow it to count as our life, which we do not have here in our hand and at our disposal but have above, hidden with him in God (Colossians 3:1 f.). If grace, the content of the Gospel, concerns us, if it is manifest and thus assumes the form of the Law, it means that we "seek the things which are above" in this quite precise sense. "The Law is spiritual" (Romans 7:14), but that means its sense and its meaning are our life's "being raised with Christ." This is what God wanted of Israel with the first as well as the second table of the Law, with the sacrifice, food and purity commandments, with the constitution as a national-church or ecclesiastical-nation, which he gave Israel as "the shadow) of things to come." This is what Jesus wanted of his disciples when he commanded them: "Love your enemies! Be careful how you give alms! Do not be anxious! Do not judge!" This is what the apostles wanted from their congregations when they admonished them to love, to unity, to purity, daily to put aside the old man. This alone can also be the meaning and content of the authority with which the Church confronts its members and the world. We are always concerned with faith in Jesus Christ, who is crucified and risen. Thus there can never be claims and demands which would have legal validity from another source or in themselves: there can only be *witnesses*. And these witnesses will always be concerned with the grace of God, which has accomplished everything for us and whose end must be this accomplishment. By saying *this*, these witnesses *admonish, warn, command, order*, and *prohibit*. They will have legal authority, because and to the extent that they proclaim the "Law of Christ" (Galatians 6:2) and thus the "Law of faith" (Romans 3:21), and thus the "Law of the Spirit of life" (Romans 8:2). And we will keep and

fulfill the Law and all its commandments if we have faith
in Jesus Christ; that means the faith which clings to him
and remains true to him, simply because he is the eternal
incarnate Word, which has accomplished all things. This
faith includes all obedience. Our works, great and small,
internal and external, are accepted if they take place as
works of this faith—and they are rejected if they do not.
We must provisionally stop at this point, for precisely this
faith, which allows Jesus Christ the right to be its representative, is the work and gift of the Holy Spirit, which we
cannot appropriate to ourselves, but for which we can only
pray.

III

We have spoken in the foregoing of the *truth* of the Gospel and the Law in their mutual relation. On this basis only
can we gain insight into their reality, of which we must
now speak.

Now we must consider what it means that the Gospel as
well as the Law—or, in our previous terms, the content and
form of the Gospel—have been put into *our* hands, into the
hands of *sinners*.

By becoming manifest, God's grace (and thus the Law)
irrefutably and unambiguously illuminates the fact and
meaning of our sinfulness. We can measure the *depth* of
our sins by the fact that nothing less than God's eternal
Word accepted us in this depth and had to do so in such a
way that he took our place, pointing us solely to faith, faith
in him who is the work and gift of the Holy Spirit! This
action also discloses the *nature* of sin, against which God
contends in Jesus Christ, the forgiveness of which he has
prepared for us in him. If this forgiveness is based on God's
doing in our place, for us, what is right in his sight, then
our sin consists in our very inability to appear for ourselves,
but still *wishing* to do so. As we have already said, sin consists in autocracy and in godlessness, inasmuch as God is

essentially gracious; but precisely our autocracy attests and means our rejection of grace and our self-assertion against God, our separation from God.

By accepting us in the gift of the Gospel and the Law, God lays this gift in our hands, in the presumptuous hands of those who, contrary to the significance and definition of this gift, desperately wish to appear on our own behalf, because we wish to assert ourselves. What will we start thereby, we who wish by all means to "start something" with everything and everyone? Notice carefully, God lays his gift in our hands *nevertheless* and, in spite of the worse than questionable purity of our hands, it is and remains *his* gift. The fourth section of this lecture discusses the *positive* meaning of this "nevertheless." But first of all, it means something *negative.* And this negative entity forms the background against which the positive one must stand out in order to be recognized as such. Thus we must speak first of the negative.

The nature of the matter requires that we turn above all now to our dealings with the *Law* of God. God's grace, by coming to us, does have the form of Law, of commandment, of requirement, of claim. What will happen if we, we sinners, perceive this claim? Paul, especially in Romans 5 and 7, gave the fundamental answer: our sin uses the Law as a springboard (ἀφορμή Romans 7:8, 11) and celebrates its resurrection (Romans 7:8 f.), becomes active and recognizable (Romans 7:7) as "sin which dwells within us" (Romans 7:20), as sinful "Law in our members" (Romans 7:23), only by winning control (Romans 5:20), by becoming "sinful beyond measure" (Romans 7:13), by producing—through misusing the Law itself—its master stroke, so to speak, distorting precisely the good, precisely the best, into its opposite (Romans 7:13), using it to deceive (Romans 7:11). Compared with it, what is the sin of the man whom the Law of God has *not* encountered? Paul, as Romans 1:18 f. shows, really took this latter sin seriously, and yet he had to call it downright "dead" (Romans 7:8) next to the sin of which the man who encounters God's law is guilty. Only in this sin is the nature of sin visible and understandable. But what is this gigantic deception which sin perpetrates by means of the Law? Paul answers: it consists in the fact that sin causes covetousness to shoot up in us, precisely in the face of the Law's "Thou shalt not covet." We must not allow ourselves to be misled to interpret this "lust" moralistically because of associations which arise in connection with the analogy of the classical *nitimur in vetitum*. . . . What we moralistically define as "lust," especially sexual libido to which the Church's exposition seems to have turned all too rapidly and all too zealously, certainly is, so Paul thinks, one of the consequences of that sin which is indeed to be taken seriously but, in comparison to what concerns us here, is "dead." The Law of which Paul speaks is indeed *spiritual*, and so, in the case of the deception which sin perpetrates by awakening that lust for what is forbidden, just as in the deception of the snake in the story of the first fall, it must be a deception relating precisely to the *spiritual* character of the Law. We derive its definition from a different passage in which Paul speaks concretely of the person deceived through sin's use of the Law. He says of the Jews who have crucified Christ and rejected him right up to the present: "They have a zeal for God, but it is unenlightened. For, being ignorant of the justification that comes from God, and seeking to establish their own, they did not submit to justification by God. For Christ is the end of the Law, for justification" (Romans 10:2 f.). This then is the lust which causes sin to shoot up within us because of the Law—precisely the lust of that scribe, who asked, "What must I do to inherit eternal life?" and whom Jesus simply reminded of the Law, of whom it is finally said, "But he desired to justify himself" (Luke 10:29). As a matter of fact, who at that time desired anything else if God's claim encountered him? This lust is human disobedience discovered at its root! For what happens when one confronted with God's claim endeavors to establish his own

86

righteousness? Apparently he makes out of God's claim a claim of his own, namely the claim that he can and will himself satisfy God's demands. Why is this disobedience? It is disobedience because God's claim bears witness to what is promised to us and fulfilled in Christ, our justification through this very Christ. *Christ* is indeed the goal of the Law and is so for our justification. It would be obedience for us to subordinate ourselves to this justification, to live a life in this subordination. But our lust shoots right past this very thing. Why? We do not recognize that the Law proclaims our justification by God. "To this day, whenever Moses is read, a veil lies over their minds" (II Corinthians 3:15). Why is this true? Why do we not know what we could still read in the Law? Precisely this is sin's deception, because we are, from the very start, engaged in asserting ourselves and advocating our cause, we conceal from ourselves the greatest thing, the decisive element in the Law, the content of which it is only the form, the healing and sanctifying grace, in order to strengthen, confirm, exalt ourselves, to represent ourselves as worthy co-workers of God, meanwhile concerned, with the help of its "letters" because they are, after all, divine letters, to observe them all and to do them justice to the best of our knowledge and in good conscience. Completely occupied with ourselves, we have made the divine "You shall be!" of the Law into the human —all too human—"You ought!" This is what Paul called the "weakening of the Law by the flesh" (Romans 8:3). To quote his converse formulation, the Law is the *power* of sin (I Corinthians 15:56). From hence, on the basis of this deception of sin, comes the "unenlightenment" of our "zeal for God." Just let no one think that, because it is based on *ignorance* and because it always is a zeal for *God*, it is a relatively harmless and forgivable zeal, perhaps to be regretted on account of its imperfection but nevertheless to be praised on account of its good intention. No, its ignorance is *disobedience*, and it is a *lie* to call it zeal for God! *Sin* triumphs in this zeal, more, infinitely more, than in what we think we know as idolatry, blasphemy, murder, adultery, and robbery; infinitely more because here, in his gift of the Law, in the misinterpreted decalogue, in the misinterpreted prophetic utterances, in the misinterpreted Solomonic wisdom, in the misinterpreted Sermon on the Mount and apostolic admonition, God himself has been made the cause and pretext of sin. Now man certainly does pounce, one on this, another on that letter and shred of the Law, with the entire passion of his caprice, victorious and left to itself by God, and at the same time with the entire passion of his bad conscience and surely, absolutely surely, taking the line of least resistance. Each pounces on that portion which he thinks he can best use and each with the triumphant thought that he, with his letter and shred in hand, sooner or later brings about—at least in the eyes of men—a kind of special justification of his own existence. Here is one in a blind frenzy of work; there is one leading an exemplary life as citizen and family man. Here is one in pursuit of "interesting" views, experiences, acquaintances, connections; there is one living with a demonstrative simplicity and frugality. Here is one engaged in the sovereign vagaries of a gypsying genius. Here is one sunk in a wrangling ecclesiastical orthodoxy and theological pedantry; there is one living in perpetually smiling evangelical freedom. Here is one involved in a busy, philanthropic, or, still better, a pedagogical welfare enterprise for all sorts of "lame ducks" among his fellow men; there is one immersed in an undertaking of far-reaching vision for world improvement on a large scale. Here is one living in the solemn whim of a private existence patterned after absolutely nothing else than his own highly individual conception; there is one living in a justice in step with the great mass and the temper of the times, and one living precisely against it, in a refined way. And here is one imbued with the fantastic plan of attempting to live for once with absolute honesty, with absolute purity, with absolute selflessness, with absolute love. Vanity of vanities! What next? In what direction can one not

88

plunge if he once ignores and bypasses the faith which God in Jesus Christ demands for himself and himself alone? There are then a thousand works of the Law, the Law torn into a thousand shreds, a thousand servitudes to which we subject ourselves, a thousand letters on each of which some little man or even many at the same time can cling in order to sip their own righteousness from it. We poor tipplers—always sipping and yet always thirsting again! A harmless, an even partly praiseworthy lust? No, for precisely this lust produces, in visible and invisible extensions of this our "good" efforts, that which, this time, not men but God, in his Law, calls idolatry, blasphemy, murder, adultery, and robbery (see Romans 2:12 f.). This our lust, this our zeal—is it for God? No, with the help and to the honor of God, it is for our own godlessness—which crucified Christ and crucifies him again and again in the midst of Christendom (Hebrews 6:6). Does this still not say enough about what it means for God to give his Law into our hands?

In order to understand what happens to the Law in this case—it is and does remain God's Law!—we must now ask the question, "What happens to the *Gospel*, which is the sense and content of the Law?" It, naturally, does not mean, for instance, that the Gospel would be completely discarded and forgotten if sin deceive us with the Law and therefore about the Law. Sin triumphs even with respect to the Law only in its misuse, not, however (for good reason, not), in its abandonment! And, on the other hand, that deception cannot mean that though the Law be misused, desecrated, corrupted, the Gospel would be preserved intact and thus that we would understand grace as grace after, as well as before. No, the content falls and is corrupted with the form, the Gospel also falls with God's Law. Of the people of Israel, which did not listen to Moses and especially to the first commandment of the Law proclaimed through Moses, which rejected and stoned its prophets, which finally crucified its Messiah, of this people, Isaiah said that they talk of nothing but "covenant" (Isaiah 8:12);

they have always known *much* and thought *highly* of God's grace, patience, and forgiveness of sins—and this is most true precisely on the day of Golgotha. The Pharisees were *far* from being as Pharisaic as we, for the sake of simplicity, imagine them. Did not they, too, wish to escape the coming wrath (Matthew 3:7)? Were not they, too, interested enough to invite Jesus to eat with them? One short and unessential step beyond them we bump into a Christianity which, with respect to the Law, has likewise fallen prey to sin's deception and thus, wishing to justify itself, no longer thinks at all about keeping that which is greatest and most decisive in the Law; nevertheless, it, too, does not ignore the Law; it, too, would like to use grace and harness grace as a counterpoise to temper its unwise zeal for God. But what does grace mean in this case? Here Jesus Christ, who gives everything to his own by himself appearing with God's majesty in their place, has become a demigod, who imparts pretended powers to them, a sort of magic talent, the presence of which can be established like that of any other talent, which they are free to control and direct as their possession, which redounds to their honor before themselves and before others, in which they believe they have a good support for their efforts to assert, to advocate, to justify themselves, with which they intend to comfort themselves (secretly, this is the most important of all), in case as a result of the incompleteness of their efforts there should be disappointments and standstills and, here and there, even simply failure. Jesus Christ becomes the indispensable companion, the useful lever arm, and finally and above all the stopgap for all our efforts toward our own justification! Jesus Christ becomes the personification of the wonderful ideas which we always invent for the sake of this justification, according to whatever the spirit and taste of our time may be! Jesus Christ becomes the great creditor who again and again is just good enough to cover the cost of our own ventures in righteousness! This is what becomes of grace, of the Gospel. In the shadow of sin's deception with the

Law, *this* must inevitably happen to the Gospel. There grace is discarded, there Christ has died in vain (Galatians 2:21), for there the offense, the saving offense of the cross, has been removed (Galatians 5:11). There we find sheer enmity against the cross (Philippians 3:18). This is the way Paul spoke of the Christianity which thrives in the shadow of this deception. It is certain that the Gospel, deformed and distorted in this way, cannot mean "the power of God for salvation" (Romans 1:16), if the deformed and distorted Law should, for instance, lead us into the temptation of which we have yet to speak. *This* Jesus Christ has not yet even helped or comforted, much less saved a single man in the temptation which must necessarily follow sin's deception.

And now we can answer the question: "If our autocracy takes possession of it, what then becomes of the Law of God under that deception of sin?"

At this point, we only touch upon the fact that in this deformation and distortion the Law is exposed to every falsification: now—that is, if we are dealing with our pretended obedience to the Law for our self-justification—natural law, or an abstract "reason," or history, or, in these recent troubled times, the "Volksnomoi" (people's laws), so happily invented, may undertake to give to the Law of God the content usable and desirable for this purpose. We only touch upon the fact that its interpretation now, if Christ is not to be its goal, will vacillate unsteadily between a *nomianism* which believes it should submit to these or those observances and disciplines, and an *antinomianism* of pure inwardness, averse to every concrete command and tie. Both nomianism and antinomianism are, of course, forms of "righteousness by works," and we only touch upon the fact, brought out by Paul in Galatians 4:8 f., that the service of the Law, robbed of promise and thereby dishonored and emptied—in plain language but in the most concrete seriousness—represents the relapse out of belief in the one living God into the impoverished *heathen worship of the elements.*

If God be not still God in his Law, then it and he have become only too similar to many other laws and many other gods which do also exist, and it will then become an enticing game to interchange him and his law with these others. Anyone who has once allowed himself to take his life in his own hand in this or that form of "righteousness by works" should, if he is wise enough, just be sure not to forget the eternal, brazen, great laws of his fate, his cosmic-sidereal antagonist, he just should not leave the calendar of his astrological possibilities for this week and for next autumn too far out of reach. It is also typical of a life under the Law which has been dishonored and emptied by our autocracy that we, like bad boys waiting for the teacher, must peer around in interstellar space, keeping a lookout for something which perhaps would still come over us and what it might mean for us. It is also typical of this our life that that calendar is really much more interesting to us than the Bible!

All of that is terrible enough, but it is still only a symptom of the much more terrible judgment which is based on the fact that *God will not be mocked* even in his dishonored and empty Law, that it remains God's claim on men, even if man subjects it to his own claims. What if God still wants his law to be fulfilled, his commandments kept? Yes, how could he fail to stand firm, how could he, as certainly as he is God, retreat from this? And what if God now takes us at our word, holds us to our bold plan and program of fulfilling his Law ourselves and in this, our fulfilling of the Law, to be our own advocates? How would it be if he would really require us to keep the smallest of his commandments even halfway, or even to a small degree? But no, God doubtless demands a total keeping of all his commandments. Now, *justify* yourself if you have been *condemned* precisely from the start and basically by thinking you can and should justify yourself! We can "have an unenlightened zeal for God" throughout our lives—and no doubt we all do just that!—but behind this stands the immovable fact (in the whole immovability of the grace of God which is apparent

92

in his Law) that God will not be deceived, that we as a whole and singly are discovered to be those who refuse him faith in order to be able to believe in ourselves and trust ourselves that much better. Behind all this stands the fact that this means judgment on all our works by which we think we can justify ourselves, and above all on the works of our faith by which we think we can justify ourselves. For if any one of our works were to be judged as sin against the first commandment, then it certainly would be the one we consider our best, the work of our faith in the Arian and Pelagian Christ, on whom we bestow the honor of just allowing him to remain the innocent useful periphery of our self-assertion. If this is the case with our best work, what about all the others? The horrible thing, which now—corresponding to sin's deception—becomes a reality between God and man, has often been described. At this point, I only mention the result: we have actually refused justification by God. Our self-justification has not succeeded because it is an impossibility. Thus we have no—no justification. I certainly can will—yes, in fact, only too well—but I cannot accomplish the good. How could I, since my very willing is, as that of a deceived deceiver, corrupt? This is what the Law, the Law we have dishonored and emptied, which still is and remains God's Law, has to say to us now. Temptation is present if we must awake from the intoxication of our lust, which shot up by virtue of sin in view of the Law, and must see that nothing has changed about the Law and its demands, if we hear again the real Law and if we now can perhaps no longer hear anything else than the real Law of God, which has *this* to say to us: you certainly can will but you cannot accomplish the good! Not only your sins, no, your good works are sinful, because, perhaps to a greater extent than those things you consider your sins, they are works of your lust *against* God!—in this moment, temptation is present. Now we only know about God's revelation that he is rightly angry with us, that to a thousand words we have not one to answer him, that we thus are lost, have fallen prey to death and hell. And what should now happen to us, since when we forfeited the Law, we forfeited also and precisely grace? This is what happens to the Law of God in our hands—it is now the "Law of sin and death" (Romans 8:2), the executor of divine wrath (Romans 4:15), the Law which Paul—not invariably but as a rule—calls the "Nomos," against service to which, against the works of which, against the righteousness of which, and against the servitude and curse of which he can only warn his congregations most urgently. This is the Law, the "office" of which he says in II Corinthians 3:2 f. is to "preach condemnation," even to "kill by the letter." This is the Law which was later so gravely mentioned in the same breath with the whore, reason, with sin and death, in fact with the devil, so urgently depicted as *the* enemy of faith, love, and hope, as *the* great antagonist of the Gospel. This is the Law of which it was said and must be said: either entirely the Law and then death, or entirely the Gospel and then life, there is no third possibility. It is the Law, dishonored and emptied by sin's deception, which, with the power of the *wrath* of God, nevertheless is and remains *his* Law. If we serve *this* Law, then there is no escape from God's judgment, and in the temptation in which this judgment is manifest, there is no counsel, no comfort, no help.

This is the negative entity which follows from the fact that God lays his gift in our hands nevertheless, in spite of our being sinners. This is *one* side of the reality of the mutual relationship of the Gospel and the Law. The Epistle to the Galatians speaks of this negative element—to be sure, not just of it, but quite emphatically also of it.

IV

We announce the *positive* element, which now and only now must be stated in view of this "nevertheless," in the words of the same Paul: "The Law intervened, so that the trespass became stronger; but where sin became stronger,

94

precisely there grace overflowed, so that as sin reigned in death, now grace reigns through justification to eternal life through Jesus Christ our Lord" (Romans 5:20 f.). For "God has consigned all men to disobedience, that he may have mercy upon all. O the depth of the riches both of the wisdom and the knowledge of God! How unsearchable are his judgments and how inscrutable are his ways! 'For who has known the mind of the Lord, or who has been his counsellor?' 'Or who has given a gift to him that he might be repaid?' For from *him* and through *him* and to *him* are all things. To *him* be glory forever. Amen" (Romans 11:32 ff.). Yes, it is unsearchable and inscrutable—it belongs to another order than that of action and reaction, merit and worthiness, it has its beginning and its end only in him —that God does lay his gift, his Word, the Gospel, and the Law in our sinful, impure hands and now that which must happen does happen: just now and only now do we rebel, we corrupt and disgrace precisely his Word, just now and now more than ever, Jesus Christ is crucified with the help and to the honor of God. But, just as the *Law* is and remains the Law of God even though dishonored and emptied by our lust, so—no, not so but still much more, God's *Gospel* is laid precisely in our sinful, unclean hands and after everything has worked itself out, just at this point, the Gospel also operates fully for the first time, it also shows itself fully for the first time for what it is, the really *glad* tidings for *real* sinners.

But is not then our real sin that we, "pursuing justification through the Law" (Romans 9:31), do not hear the Gospel in the Law, do not wish to allow Christ to be the end of the Law? What kind of power can one expect grace to have if we scorned and despised, even hated it? To this, we must answer: God is God. Power, the power of the resurrection (Philippians 3:10) belongs, in any case, precisely and in the first place to grace, which we scorned and despised, even hated; belongs to the Christ, who to this very day has been delivered into the hands of sinners, crucified, dead and buried. "Behold, I make all things new!" Before this "I" no flesh, really none, should be able to boast, not even of its non-resistance! Its regeneration begins precisely at that point at which, as far as we are concerned, absolutely nothing else is real than that we compromise ourselves before him and for him, that point at which the phrase, "I do *not* nullify the grace of God" (Galatians 2:21) can only pass our lips as the acknowledgment of a gift and a miracle which happens to us, and with the acknowledgment, "I am the most distinguished of sinners" (I Timothy 1:15). Precisely and only for this most distinguished sin in all of us, for the sin which became inordinately sinful as the sin against his very person, Jesus became a man, died, and rose again. And thus the victory of the Gospel, the victory of grace is precisely God's victory over this *real* sin, over the sin of our misuse of the *Law*, the sin of our *unbelief*.

We shall have to consider this unsearchable, this inscrutable victory, this victory whose honor is the honor of God, from three points of view:

In the first place, the grace of God, Jesus Christ himself, converts precisely the *judgment*, under which the misused and yet valid law of God places us, into our *justification*. He reveals himself as the Saviour through the Law also in this shape. He vivifies through the Gospel in which he kills through the Law. Now this order, "Law and Gospel," becomes legitimate and meaningful! Through the *content* of the Gospel, thus through himself, he awakens, to the life of faith in him as the one who justifies us, our very existence, which was, through the form of the Gospel, through the Law, condemned and expelled into hell because of our unbelief, our existence as it is in all its nakedness and ugliness, thus including our unbelief. This is true in spite of the fact that we are sinners from head to toe, in our heart and in our deeds—no, precisely because we stand before him thus and only thus! We must emphasize that free grace, Jesus Christ himself, does that. We could not do it ourselves, as

96

certainly as we do not have in us what it takes, and as certainly as we are still much less able to bestow it on ourselves from outside ourselves. Our justification in the judgment also does not, however, occur on the strength of an immanent lawfulness, as that by which night and day, winter and spring, pain and joy, anxiety and rest follow each other, or in the prudence of the function of a mechanism once arranged in a definite way, or according to the rule of that Absolute Spirit which through Thesis and Antithesis finally returns to itself. The order Law-Gospel, sin-righteousness, which here concerns us is characterized by its identity with the order death-life. But that means it is entirely unintelligible to us as an order. It can only be event and *fact* and we can of ourselves believe it only as the promise of what Jesus Christ does for us, and our belief will be a source of amazement to us. We shall only *really* be able to believe, without knowing whether what we are thus doing is possible. And if Jesus Christ becomes manifest to us through the Law which judges us, if the Law thus becomes the disciplinarian preparing us for him (Galatians 3:24), if we, who amaze ourselves, believe *in him* in our unbelief and despite our unbelief, then this our faith certainly contains in it the decisive knowledge of our sin and the certainty of its forgiveness; but as our faith can now, as faith, only wish to be faith *in him*, as it lives and has its being entirely in him as its object and in no sense in itself, so also our awareness of sin and certainty of forgiveness, and thus our certainty of salvation, become absolutely nothing else than knowledge and certainty *coming from him*, and cannot in any sense be a knowledge and certainty based on themselves and thus knowledge and certainty resulting in any sort of praise for us. The victorious Gospel is the power of God for salvation to everyone who has faith (Romans 1:16). Thus and only thus is it the really *victorious* Gospel despite our sinful, unclean hands.

In the second place, the grace of God, Jesus Christ himself, makes us free from that "Law of sin and death" (Ro-

mans 8:2). If we are, as the victorious Gospel tells us, justified in him, without ourselves and against ourselves, against
our disobedience and unbelief, then that still means that
this Law cannot condemn us on account of our disobedience and unbelief. Even as "the Law of sin and death," it
has the right and power to condemn us only because it is
God's Law. But if God is for us, has confined us in unbelief in order to ha:e mercy upon us, just this way, precisely in the form of an awakening of the dead, who can
be against us? Certainly not the right and power of his own
Law! Our double anxiety before the Law is now thus also
cast into that confinement of our unbelief: both the anxiety
before its letters, whether or not we know them all and
whether or not we intend to do them justice, and the anxiety
before the consequences of the fact that we certainly are
disobedient to the whole of it because we do not believe—
taken together, the two parts of this double anxiety make
up our fear of life. *It shall no longer be!* God's mercy bends
over that confinement into which this anxiety is cast and
that means that this anxiety can now only be one overcome,
comforted, set at rest, surrounded by a solid shore of hope
and joy. But this liberation reaches deeper: if God's Law
does not really condemn us, then it *is* by no means any
longer the "Law of sin and death"! If the Gospel triumphs,
it not only re-establishes itself as overflowing grace, overflowing precisely on its enemies—no, then the *Law*, the
form of the Gospel also is re-established out of the letters to
the totality of its words, of its one single Word, out of the
demand, "You ought!" to the promise, "You shall be!", out
of the claim on our accomplishment to the claim on our
trust. Then the Law no longer speaks as the instrument of
sin's deception and as the organ of God's wrath, but in its
proper original sense as witness, as the revelation of him
who does all things well and asks nothing from us except
that we believe he *will* do all things well. Because the victory of the Gospel also means that, we read expressly in
Romans 7–8 that we have been set free in Christ Jesus

"through the Law of the Spirit of life." Let us note well, all that in Christ Jesus! In our liberation, we honor the glory of *his* work. In order to see our liberation, we can only gaze on *him*. In order to be thankful for it, we can only wish to praise *him*. In order to enjoy it, we can only depend on *him*. Aside from him and without him, apart from the mercy of God which he himself is, which bends over us, we remain confined in disobedience, deceived deceivers, in condemnation and the shadow of death afterward just as before. *He* is our freedom. *He* is the victorious Gospel also in this respect, but he *is* it.

In the third place, the grace of God, Jesus Christ himself, gives us what we need so that our justification and liberation which have been accomplished in him may also be a reality in us: the Holy Spirit of power, of love and self-control (II Timothy 1:7). It gives us the Spirit of *power* to depend on him in an ultimately imperturbable clarity and truth, to depend on him and to remain in him, although, no, precisely because, we must recognize that we are entirely incapable of that. It gives us the Spirit of *love* for him who is the fulfillment of the Law (Romans 13:10) because love allows us, together with all his people bearing each other's burden (Galatians 6:2) and thus also united with him, to gaze on his revealed will, as the bride gazes at the bridegroom, although, no, precisely because, of ourselves we love neither him nor our neighbor. It gives us, finally, the Spirit of *self-control*, which shall always preserve us from forgetting this "although" and "because," from forgetting that, after as before, we ourselves want, to our own ruin, to be like God, knowing good and evil, the self-control which will drive us thus again and again to look and listen to him as our Saviour. This gift of the Holy Spirit is no magic, no enchantment. Anyone who can interpret it thus does not know it. It is, quite wonderfully but also quite soberly, our transfer to the place and status of those in whose defeat the victory of the Gospel, and thereby our justification and thereby the revelation of the Law as

99

the "Law of the Spirit of life," has become real. One will always recognize those who have the Holy Spirit by the fact that they recognize themselves as those who are *poor* before God. These who are, in this sense, poor in spirit (Matthew 5:3) are those in whose sinful, unclean hands the Gospel and the Law have been laid, not in vain but for their salvation, because, through the body of Christ crucified for us and his blood shed for us, they are fed and satisfied and sustained unto eternal life.

CHURCH AND STATE

INTRODUCTION

The title "Justification and Justice"* indicates the question with which I am dealing in this work.

First of all, I will state the question thus: is there a connection between justification of the sinner through faith alone, completed once for all by God through Jesus Christ, and the problem of justice, the problem of human law? Is there an inward and vital connection by means of which in any sense human justice (or law), as well as divine justification, becomes a concern of Christian faith and Christian responsibility, and therefore also a matter which concerns the Christian Church? But we may clearly ask the same question with reference to other conceptions; take the problem of *order*, for instance, of that order which is no longer, or not yet, the order of the Kingdom of God; or the problem of *peace*, which is no longer, or not yet, the eternal Peace of God; or the problem of *freedom*, which is no longer, or not yet, the freedom of the Children of God—do all these problems belong to the realm of the "new creation" of man through the Word of God, do they all belong to his sanctification through the Spirit? Is there, in spite of all differences, an inner and vital connection between the service of God in Christian living indicated in James 1:27 and what we are accustomed to call "Divine Service" in the worship of the Church as such, and another form of service,

* The German title is *Rechtfertigung und Recht.*—ED.

what may be described as a "political" service of God, a
service of God which, in general terms, would consist in
the careful examination of all those problems which are
raised by the existence of human justice, of law, or, rather,
which would consist in the recognition, support, defence,
and extension of this law—and all this, not in spite of but
because of divine justification? In what sense can we, may
we, and must we follow Zwingli, who, in order to distinguish them and yet to unite them, speaks in the same breath
of "divine and human justice"?

It should be noted that the interest in this question begins where the interest in the Reformation confessional writings and Reformation theology as a whole ceases, or rather,
to put it more exactly, where it begins to fade.[1] The fact
that both realities exist: divine justification and human justice, the proclamation of Jesus Christ, faith in Him and the
office and authority of the secular power, the mission of
the Church and the mission of the State, the hidden life of
the Christian in God and also his duty as a citizen—all this
has been clearly and powerfully emphasized for us by the
Reformers. And they also took great pains to make it clear
that the two are not in conflict, but that they can very well
exist side by side, each being competent in its own sphere.
But it must be strongly emphasized that on this point they
do not by any means tell us all that we might have expected—not excepting Luther in his work *Of Worldly Authority* of 1523 or Calvin in the majestic closing chapters
of his *Institutio*. Clearly we need to know not only that the
two are not in conflict, but, first and foremost, to what extent they are connected. To this question, the question as
to the relationship between that which they maintained
here (with the greatest polemical emphasis), and the *centre* of their Christian message, we receive from the Reformers either no answer at all, or, at the best, a very inadequate

[1] Cf. the instructive composition of H. Obendiek: *Die Obrigkeit nach dem Bekenntnis der reformierten Kirche*, Munich,
1936.

answer. Whatever our attitude may be to the content of that last chapter of the *Institutio,* *"De Politica Administratione"* (and, so far as we are concerned, we are prepared to take a very positive position), this at least is clear, that as we look back on the earlier parts of the work, and in particular on the second and third books and their cardinal statements about Jesus Christ, the Holy Spirit, sin and grace, faith and repentance, we feel like a traveller, suddenly transported to a distant land, who is looking back at the country from which he started. For on the question of how far the *politica administratio* in the title of the fourth book belongs to the *externis mediis vel adminiculis quibus Deus in Christi societatem nos invitat et in ea retinet* we shall find only the most scattered instruction, for all the richness which the book otherwise contains. But the same is true of the corresponding theses of Luther and Zwingli, and of those of the Lutheran and Reformed Confessional writings. That authority and law rest on a particular *ordinatio* of divine providence, necessary on account of unconquered sin, serving to protect humanity from the most concrete expressions and consequences of that sin, and thus to be accepted by humanity with gratitude and honour— these are certainly true and biblical thoughts, but they are not enough to make clear the relationship between this issue and the other, which the Reformation held to be the decisive and final issue of faith and confession. What does Calvin mean when, on the one hand, he assures us: *"spirituale Christi regnum et civilem ordinationem res esse plurimum sepositas"*[2]—and on the other hand twice[3] points to the subjection of all earthly rulers to *Christ,* indicated in the passage, Psalms 2:10 ff., and describes the ideal outcome of that divine *ordinatio* as the *politia Christiana?*[4] How far *Christiana?* What has Christ to do with this matter? we ask, and we are left without any real answer, as

[2] *Inst.* IV., 20, 1.
[3] *Ibid.,* 20, 5, and 29.
[4] *Ibid.,* 20, 14.

though a particular ruling of a general, somewhat anonymous Providence were here the last word. And if we read Zwingli's strong statement,[5] that the secular power has "strength and assurance from the teaching and action of Christ," the disappointing explanation of this statement consists only in the fact that in Matthew 22:21 Christ ordained that we should render unto Caesar the things which are Caesar's and unto God the things which are God's, and that by paying the customary "tribute money" (*Didrachmon:* Matthew 17:24 f.) he himself confirmed this teaching. That is again quite true in itself,[6] but, when stated thus apart from its context, in spite of the appeal to the text of the Gospel, it is based not on the Gospel but on the Law.

We can neither overlook nor take lightly this gap in the teaching that we have received from the fathers of our church—the lack of a gospel foundation, that is to say, in the strictest sense, of a Christological foundation, for this part of their creed. There is, of course, no question that here, too, they wished to expound only the teaching of the Bible. But the question remains: in introducing these biblical data into their creed, were they regulating their teaching by the standard which elsewhere they considered final? That is, were they founding law on justice or justification? political power on the power of Christ? Or were they not secretly building on another foundation, and, in so doing, in spite of all their apparent fidelity to the Bible, were they not actually either ignoring or misconstruing the fundamental truth of the Bible?

Let us consider what would happen if that were so: if the thought of human justice were merely clamped on to the truth of divine justification, instead of being vitally connected with it. On the one hand, to a certain extent it would be possible to purify the truth of divine justification from

[5] *Schlussreden*, Art. 35.

[6] Matthew 17, dealing as it does with a Temple tax, does not really belong here.

this foreign addition and to build upon it a highly spiritual
message and a very spiritual Church, which would claim
to expect "everything from God," in a most devout spirit,
and yet, in actual fact, would dispute this "everything" because, by their exclusive emphasis upon the Kingdom of
God, forgiveness of sins and sanctification, they had ceased
to seek or find any entrance into the sphere of these problems of human justice. On the other hand, it would be possible to consider the question of human law very seriously
(still, perhaps, in relation to the general divine providence,
but freed from the Reformers' juxtaposition of human justice and divine justification) and to construct a secular
gospel of human law and a secular church, in which, in
spite of emphatic references to "God," it would inevitably
become clear that this Deity is not the Father of our Lord
Jesus Christ, and that the human justice which is proclaimed is in no sense the Justice of God. Since the Reformation it is evident that these two possibilities—and with
them Pietistic sterility on one hand, and the sterility of the
Enlightenment on the other—have been realized in many
spheres. But it cannot be denied that there is a connection
between this fact and that gap in the Reformers' teaching.

And now we live to-day at a time when, in the realm of
the Church, the question of divine justification and, in the
realm of the State, the question of human law are being
raised with new emphasis, and we seem, now as then, to
be pressing onward towards developments that cannot yet
be foreseen. It is obvious to recall that both justification
and justice, or the Kingdom of Christ and the kingdoms of
this world, or the Church and the State, formerly stood
side by side in the Reformation confession, and that by
"worship in spirit and in truth" the Reformers understood
a life in both these realms. But if we are not once more to
drift into sterile and dangerous separations, it will not be
enough to recollect the Reformation, to repeat the formulae
in which it placed the two realms side by side, to recite
over and again (with more or less historical accuracy and

sympathetic feeling) "the Reformed conception of the State" and the like, as though that gap were not evident, as though the Reformation teaching did not, with that gap, bear within itself the temptation to those separations. If the intensity of our present situation is to be our salvation and not our ruin, then the question which we asked at the outset must be put: is there an actual, and therefore inward and vital, connection between the two realms?

What is offered here is a study—a biblical, or more exactly, a New Testament study—for the answer to this question. For the dubious character of the Reformation solution is decidedly due to the questionable character of the authoritative scriptural arguments on this subject presented at that time. If we are to progress further to-day, we must at all costs go back to the Scriptures. This pamphlet represents a partial attempt in this direction.[7]

I shall begin by reproducing in a few sentences what is, as far as I can see, the latest important statement of theological thought upon this subject: the work presented on our theme by K. L. Schmidt in his Basle inaugural lecture of December 2, 1936, under the title, "The Conflict of Church and State in the New Testament Community."[8]

[7] The reader will do well to note that in this book one thing only is attempted: to move along the road of exegesis towards a better view of the problem "Church and State." It would in my opinion be a great advantage if some were to admit that such an attempt is necessary.

[8] *Theologische Blätter*, 1937, No. 1. Since the completion of this work I have encountered Gerhard Rittel, *Das Urteil des neuen Testaments über den Staat* (*Zeitschr. f. Syst. Theol.*, 14 Jahrg. 1937, pp. 651–80, published in June 1938). It throws no new light on the subject with which I am concerned. On p. 665 of the essay we are asked to consider carefully "whether our exegesis is *true* exegesis, that is, whether its only goal is to discover what is given in the text or whether the writer's own wishes have—perhaps unconsciously—been introduced." Now this is a warning that can always be heard to advantage. Only we are also entitled to ask for some restraint in their apostrophizing of others from those who cannot themselves be certain as to what

The fundamental teaching of the Church on her relation to the State is "the harsh picture of the execution of Jesus Christ by the officials of the State." What is this State? It is one of those angelic powers (ἐξουσίαι) of this age, which is always threatened by "demonization," that is, by the temptation of making itself an absolute. And, over against this State, what is the Church? It is the actual community (πολίτευμα) of the new Heaven and the new Earth, as such here and now certainly still hidden, and therefore in the realm of the State a foreign community (παροικία). But the solidarity of distress and death unites Christians with all men, and so also with those who wield political power. Even though the Church prefers to suffer persecution at the hands of the State, which has become a "beast out of the pit of the abyss," rather than take part in the deification of Caesar, yet it still knows that it is responsible for the State and for Caesar, and it finally manifests this responsibility, "the prophetic service of the Church as Watchman," in its highest form by praying for the State and for its officials in all circumstances.

Schmidt's presentation is explicitly confined to one section only of the problem of the "Church and State in the New Testament," namely, with the question that appears to be directly opposed to ours: the question of the *conflict* between the two realms. But it seems to me important to determine that even in this other aspect of the problem, investigation of the New Testament inevitably reveals a whole series of view-points which are of the highest importance for the answer to our question about the *positive* connection between the two realms. This is so clear that in what follows I shall confine myself simply to the order traced by Schmidt.

---

they *must*, and what they *may not*, say on this subject. On p. 652, for example, the statements and the omissions on the subject of the "Fremdstaat" and the "Volksstaat" may well be as closely related to the "wishes" of the author as to those of certain "principalities and powers."

I. THE CHURCH AND THE STATE AS THEY
CONFRONT ONE ANOTHER

I, too, consider it right and important to point first of all to the situation in which *Jesus* and *Pilate* confront one another. So far as I can see, the Reformation writers in their teaching about Church and State, among all the somewhat significant Gospel texts that are concerned with this encounter, were interested only in the words of John 18:36: "My Kingdom is not of this world." Their thoughts about the Electoral Prince of Saxony or the Council of Zürich or Geneva would clearly have been disturbed, had they concentrated intensively upon the person of Pilate. But did the Reformers see clearly at this point? Is a "disturbance" all that can be expected? Might they not perhaps have found here a better foundation for what they wished to say on this matter? Here, at any rate, we must try to fill up the gap which they have left.[9]

[9] In the following passage I have found Calvin's views on the *sub Pontio Pilato* of the creed most illuminating. The passage is actually set in a quite different context.

Pourquoy n'est il dict simplement en un mot qu'il est mort, mais est parté de Ponce Pilate, soutsz lequel il a souffert?

Cela n'est pas seulement pour nous asseurer de la certitude de l'histoire: mais aussi pour signifier, que sa mort emporte condemnation.

Comment cela?

Il est mort, pour souffrir la peiene qui nous estoit deue, et par ce moyen nous en delivrer. Or pource que nous estions coulpables devant le jugement de Dieu comme mal-faicteurs: pour representer nostre personne, il a voulu comparoistre devant le siege d'un iuge terrien, et estre condamné par la bouche d'iceluy: pour nous absoudre au throne du Juge celeste.

Neantmoins Pilate le prononce innocent et ainsi il ne le condamné pas, comme s'il en estoit digne (Matth. xxvii. 24; Luc. xxiii. 14).

Il y a l'un et l'autre. C'est qu'il est justife par le temoignage du juge, pour monstrer, qu'il ne souffre point pour ses demerites, mais pour les nostres: et cependant est condamné solennellement

In point of fact, in this encounter two points stand out with an almost blinding clarity: the State, in its "demonic" form, and thus its authority as the "power of the present age," on the one hand; the homelessness of the Church in this age, on the other hand. If the "rulers[10] of this world" had recognized the wisdom of God, which "we," the apostles, speak to the perfect, then "they would not have crucified the Lord of Glory" (I Corinthians 2:6 f.). There they showed that they did not recognize the wisdom of God. But the teaching on the separation between Church and State was not, and is not, the only teaching which the Church may glean from the passages concerned with the encounter between Jesus and Pilate.

I turn next to John 19:2; here Jesus expressly confirms Pilate's claim to have "power" over Him, and not, indeed, an accidental or presumptuous power, but one given to him "from above."[11] And this power is in no sense in itself, and as such, a power of the Evil One, of enmity to Jesus and His claims. Pilate himself formulated the matter thus in the

---

par la sentence d'iceluy mesme, pour denoter, qu'il est vrayment nostre pleige, recevant la condamnation pour nous afin de nous en acquiter.

C'est bien dit. Car s'il estoit pecheur il ne seroit pas capable de souffrir la mort pour les autres: et neantmoins, afin que sa condamnation nous soit delivrance, il faut qu'il soit repute entre les iniques (Jes. liii. 12).

Je l'entens ainsi.

(Catéchisme de l'Eglise de Genève, 1542. *Bekenntnisschriften der nach Gottes Wort reformierter Kirchen*, Munich, 1937 f. Vol. I., p. 9.)

[10] "Archontes" is the title given in Romans 13:3 to the officials of the State!

[11] In view of this passage, it seems to me impossible to say, as does Schlier (*Die Beurteilung des Staates im neuen Testament*, 1932, p. 312): "The earthly State cannot possibly pronounce judgment on this Kingdom and its representatives." It was clearly called to do so through the synagogue of the old Covenant (and, in the sense in which the Gospels use the words, it was certainly called to do so "non sine deo").

previous verse 10: "I have power to release thee and power to crucify thee." As power given by God, it could be used either way towards Jesus without losing its divine character. Certainly, had Jesus been released by Pilate, that would not have meant that the claim of Jesus to be King would have been recognized. Who for this end was born, and for this end came into the world, that He should bear witness to the truth (John 18:37). Such "recognition" cannot be and is not Pilate's business. To the question of truth, the State is neutral. "What is truth?" But the release of Jesus, and with it the recognition by the "rulers of this world" of the wisdom of God, might have meant the possibility of proclaiming openly the claim of Jesus to be such a king; or, in other words, it would have meant the legal granting of the right to preach justification! Now Pilate did *not* release Jesus. He used his power to crucify Jesus. Yet Jesus expressly acknowledged that even so his power was given him by God. Did He thereby, in the mind of the evangelist, subject Himself to the will and the verdict of a general divine providence? Or does the evangelist mean that in the use Pilate made of his power, instead of giving a just judgment, actually, under the cloak of legality, he allowed injustice to run its course? Was the one thing, or at least the chief thing, he wanted to emphasize here: that the State, by this decision, turned against the Church?

No; what he means is that what actually took place in this use of the statesman's power was the only possible thing that could take place in the fulfilment of the gracious will of the Father of Jesus Christ! Even at the moment when Pilate (still in the garb of justice! and in the exercise of the power given him by God) allowed injustice to run its course, he was the human created instrument of that justification of sinful man that was completed once for all time through that very crucifixion.

Consider the obvious significance of the whole process in the light of the Pauline message: when Pilate takes Jesus from the hands of the Jews in order to have Him scourged and crucified, he is, so to say, the middleman who takes Him over in the name of paganism, who in so doing declares the solidarity of paganism with the sin of Israel, but in so doing also enters into the inheritance of the promise made to Israel. What would be the worth of all the legal protection which the State could and should have granted the Church at that moment, compared with this act in which, humanly speaking, the Roman governor became the virtual founder of the Church? Was not this claim confirmed, for example, in the testimony of the centurion at the Cross (Mark 15:39) which anticipates all the creeds of Christendom? Then there is another truth which the Church might *also* gather from the meeting of Jesus and Pilate; namely, the very State which is "demonic" may will evil, and yet, in an outstanding way, may be constrained to do good. The State, even in this "demonic" form, cannot help rendering the service it is meant to render. It can no more evade it in the incident recorded by Luke 13:1–5, where the same Pilate, the murderer of young Galileans, becomes at the same time the instrument of the call to repentance, in the same way as the—equally murderous—Tower of Siloam. This is why the State cannot lose the honour that is its due. For that very reason the New Testament ordains that in all circumstances honour must be shown to its representatives (Romans 13:1–8; I Peter 2:17).

The synoptic accounts of the Barabbas episode point in the same direction. What is Pilate doing when he releases the "notable" Barabbas, cast into "prison for insurrection and murder," but delivers "to scourging and crucifixion" the Jesus whom he has himself declared to be guiltless? For all our amazement at such justice, we may not overlook the fact that in that very act of the political authority, not one of the earliest readers of the Gospels could think of anything other than that act of God, in which He "made Him to be sin for us, who knew no sin, that we might be made the righteousness of God in Him" (II Corinthians 5:21). What is this extremely unjust human judge doing at this point? In an eminent and direct way he is fulfilling the word of the supremely just Divine Judge. Where would the Church be if this released Barabbas were in the place of the guiltless Jesus? if, that is, there had been no "demonic" State?

Finally, there is one other point in the passages referring to Pilate which must not be overlooked: Jesus was *not* condemned as an enemy of the State, as the "King of the Jews" —although, according to Matthew 27:11; Mark 15:2, He acknowledged Himself to be a king.[12] Strictly speaking, Jesus was never condemned at all. All four evangelists vie with one another in contending that Pilate declared Him innocent, that he regarded Him as "a just man" (Matthew 27:19–24; Mark 15:14; Luke 23:14, 15, 22; John 18:38; 19:4, 6).[13] Here, too, the connection with justification now becomes clear: this same Pilate, constrained to become the instrument of the death of Jesus, ordained by God for the justification of sinful man—this same Pilate is also forced to confirm the presupposition of this event: to affirm expressly and openly the innocence of Christ, and—of course —it is in this very fact that he is fulfilling his specific function. "Pilate sought to release Him" (John 19:12). For it is in this sentence of acquittal (which he did *not* pro-

---

[12] It is not correct to say that Jesus "fell a victim to a political charge." (G. Dehn, "Engel und Obrigkeit," *Theologische Aufsätze*, 1936, p. 91.)

[13] I am indebted to Professor Ernst Wolf of Halle for the following: "On Ash Wednesday the Emperor kisses and gives gifts to the children of his orphanages; later in the procession, in the presence of the whole people, he enfeoffs or rather burdens the Minister of Justice with the 'Inkwell of Pilate,' and as he lays it on the neck of the bowing man he says 'Judge with justice like him.'" A direct reminder of the scrupulously correct behaviour of Roman justice in matters pertaining to this mystery did not seem to the successors in the Imperium Romanum out of place in Holy Week; to Syrians and Abyssinians the "Landpfleger" and his spouse Procla were almost holy beings. ("Sir Galahad," Byzanz. *Von Kaisern, Engeln und Eunuchen*, 1937, E. P. Tal and Co., Vienna, pp. 87–88.)

nounce) that his duty lies. If he had done so, the State would have shown its *true* face. Had it really done so, then acquittal would have had to follow, and the State would have had to grant legal protection to the Church! The fact that this did not actually happen is clearly regarded by the Evangelists as a deviation from the line of duty on the part of Pilate, as a failure on the part of the State. Pilate "delivered" Jesus to crucifixion, because he wished to satisfy the people (Mark 15:15). The political charge against Jesus was for Pilate clearly groundless, but he "gave sentence that it should be as they required" (Luke 23:24). "Take *ye* him and crucify him!" (John 19:6). This decision has nothing to do with the law of the State nor with the administration of justice. The Jews themselves confirmed this: "*We* have a law and by *our* law he ought to die" (John 19:7). It was not in accordance with the law of the State, but *in spite* of this law, and in accordance with a totally *different* law, and in flagrant defiance of justice, that Jesus had to die. "Ye, the Jews, have killed Jesus!" is the cry throughout the New Testament, with the exception of I Corinthians 2:8 (Acts 2:23; 3:15; 7:52; I Thessalonians 2:15). In this encounter of Pilate and Jesus the "demonic" State does not assert itself too much but too little; it is a State which at the decisive moment fails to be true to itself. Is the State here an absolute? If only Pilate had taken himself absolutely seriously as a representative of the State he would have made a different use of his power. Yet the fact that he used it as he did could not alter the fact that this power was really given him "from above." But he could not use it as he did without contradicting his true function; under the cloak of legality he trampled on the law which he should have upheld; in so doing, however, it became evident that if he had been true to his commission he would have had to decide otherwise. Certainly, in deflecting the course of justice he became the involuntary agent and herald of divine justification; yet at the same time he makes it clear that real human justice, a real exposure of the true face of the State, would inevitably have meant the recognition of the right to proclaim divine justification, the Kingdom of Christ which is not of this world, freely and deliberately.

We must not again lose sight of this doubly positive determination of the encounter between these two realms, as it has emerged in this critical instance. Particularly in considering this most critical instance we cannot say that the legal administration of the State "has nothing to do with the order of Redemption"; that here we have been moving in the realm of the first and not of the second article of the Creed.[14] No, Pontius Pilate now belongs not only to the Creed but to its second article in particular!

II. THE ESSENCE OF THE STATE

Turning to the exegesis of the passage Romans 13:1–7, which has been so much studied in every age, it may be thought peculiar that although an ancient explanation mentioned by Irenaeus[15] was clearly not generally accepted, yet in recent years fresh emphasis has been laid[16] on the fact that the word ἐξουσίαι, which is used by Paul in verse 1, and in Titus 3:1 and also by Luke, to indicate political authority is used throughout the rest of the New Testament, wherever it appears, in the plural (or in the singular with πᾶσα) (I Corinthians 15:24; Colossians 1:16; 2:10, 15; Ephesians 1:21; 3:10; 6:12; I Peter 3:22) to indicate a group of those angelic powers which are so characteristic of the biblical conception of the world and of man. ἐξουσίαι, like ἀρχαί or ἄρχοντες, δυνάμεις, θρόνοι, κυριότητες, ἄγγελοι, etc., and all these entities

[14] G. Dehn, op. cit., pp. 97 and 106.
[15] Adv. o.h. V. 24, I.
[16] Was H. Schlier ("Machte und Gewalten im neuen Testament," *Theologische Blätter*, 292) the first to express this? G. Dehn was in any case the first to develop the argument to any great extent.

which are so difficult to distinguish (probably they should
all be included under the comprehensive heading ἄγγελοι)
constitute created, but invisible, spiritual and heavenly
powers, which exercise, in and above the rest of creation,
a certain independence, and in this independence have a
certain superior dignity, task, and function, and exert a certain real influence.

The researches of G. Dehn strengthen the already strong
probability which arises from the language itself, that when
the Church of the New Testament spoke of the State, the
emperor or king, and of his representatives and their activities, it had in mind the picture of an "angelic power"
of this kind, represented by this State and active within it.
We have already met the concept ἐξουσία in the singular
as indicating the power given to Pilate, to crucify Jesus or
to release Him. Similarly, the concept ἄρχοντες (I Corinthians 2:8) is certainly intended to designate the State
—and an angelic power.[17] What does this mean? It has
been rightly maintained[18] that this explains how it came
to pass that the State, from being the defender of the law,
established by God's will and ordinance, could become "the
beast out of the abyss" of Revelation 13,[19] dominated by
the Dragon, demanding the worship of Caesar, making war
on the Saints, blaspheming God, conquering the entire
world. An angelic power may indeed become wild, degen-
erate, perverted, and so become a "demonic" power. That,
clearly, had happened with the State as represented by
Pilate which crucified Jesus. When Paul warns the Colos-
sian Christians against the seductions of these angelic powers which have become "demonic," against a "worshipping
of angels" (Colossians 2:18), when he exhorts them to

[17] And according to Rom. viii. 39 (οὔτε τις κτίσις ἑτέρα)
we may not be far from the truth of the matter in describing
the State as an ανθρωπίνη κτίσις (I Pet. ii. 13).

[18] Cf. G. Dehn, op. cit., p. 108.

[19] Cf. H. Schlier, "Vom Antichrist," *Theologische Aufsätze,*
1936, p. 110 f.

strive not with flesh and blood but with principalities and powers, with "rulers of the darkness of this world" (Ephesians 6:12), when he comforts them by the assurance that these "powers" cannot separate us from the love of Christ (Romans 8:38 f.),[20] and when he gives the vision of their ultimate "deliverance" through Christ in His parousia (I Corinthians 15:24)—all this may have a more or less direct bearing upon the "demons" and the "demonic" forces in the political sphere.

But the last passage which was quoted also contains a warning. When the separation between Christ and the State has been established, the last word on the vision of the "beast out of the abyss" has not been said. I think it is dangerous to translate the word καταργεῖν in I Corinthians 15:24 as "annihilate"—however clearly it bears that meaning in other passages. For immediately afterwards, in verse 25, the passage runs: "He must reign till He hath put all His enemies under His feet"—that is, till He has sovereign power over them. But that is also the image used in Philippians 2:9 f.—"Wherefore God also hath highly exalted Him, and given Him a name which is above every name; that at the name of Jesus every knee should bow, of things in Heaven and things in earth and things under the earth"; in Ephesians 1:20, 21—"He set Him at His own right hand in the heavenly places far above all principality and power and might. . . ."; in I Peter 3:22—"Who is gone into heaven and is on the right hand of God; angels and authorities and powers being made subject unto Him." The same image, too, is used in that particularly striking passage: Colossians 2:15: "Having spoiled principalities and powers, He made a show of them openly, triumphing over them in it." The destiny of the rebellious angelic powers which is made clear in Christ's resurrection and parousia is not that they will be annihilated, but that they will be forced into the service and the glorification of Christ, and,

[20] I am surprised that G. Dehn (op. cit., p. 101) maintains the opposite point of view.

through Him, of God. And both the beginning and the middle of their story also correspond to this ultimate destiny. I fail to see how one can say[21] without further ado that they simply represent "the world which lives on itself and by itself and as such is the antipodes and exact opposite of the creation": "In them the solitary world arises." According to Colossians 1:15 it is rather the case that they have been created in the Son of God as in the image of the invisible God, by Him and unto Him, and further, according to Colossians 2:10, that in Him they have their Head. From the first, then, they do not belong to themselves. From the first they stand at the disposal of Jesus Christ. To them, too, His work is relevant: "He was seen of angels" (I Timothy 3:16). The outcome of St. Paul's preaching to the heathen is that through the existence of the Church the "manifold wisdom of God"[22] might be made known unto them (Ephesians 3:10). With the Church they, too, desire to gaze into the mystery of the salvation which is to be revealed in the future (I Peter 1:12). And they are present not only as spectators; for them, too, the peace won by the crucifixion of Christ (Colossians 1:20) and the ἀνακεφαλαίωσις (Ephesians 1:10) are in both passages related both to earth and to heaven. We should note that here there is no question of any justification of the "demons" and the "demonic" forces; nor is the function of Christ concerning the angelic powers directly connected with divine justification. But it seems to have some connection with human justice. For what seems to be meant here is that in Christ the angelic powers are called to order and, so far as they need it, they are restored to their original order. Therefore any further rebellion in this realm can, in principle, only take place in accordance with their creation, and within Christ's order, in the form of unwilling service to the Kingdom of Christ, until even that rebellion, within the boundaries of the King-

[21] With H. Schlier, *Machte und Gewalten*, op. cit., p. 291.
[22] Probably Colossians 1:26 may also belong here.

dom of Christ, is broken down in His resurrection and parousia. At the present time, in the period bounded by the resurrection and the parousia, there is no further rebellion of the heavenly powers; no longer can they escape from their original order.

What follows when all this is applied to the political angelic power? Clearly this: that that power, the State as such, belongs originally and ultimately to Jesus Christ; that in its comparatively independent substance, in its dignity, its function, and its purpose, it should serve the Person and the Work of Jesus Christ and therefore the justification of the sinner. The State can of course become "demonic," and the New Testament makes no attempt to conceal the fact that at all times the Church may, and actually does, have to deal with the "demonic" State. From this point of view the State becomes "demonic" not so much by an unwarrantable assumption of autonomy—as is often assumed—as by the *loss* of its legitimate, relative *independence,* as by a renunciation of its true substance, dignity, function, and purpose, a renunciation which works out in Caesar worship, the myth of the State, and the like. We should add that, in the view of the New Testament, in *no* circumstances can this "demonic" State finally achieve what it desires; with gnashing of teeth it will have to serve where it wants to dominate; it will have to build where it wishes to destroy; it will have to testify to God's justice where it wishes to display the injustice of men.

On the other hand, it is not inevitable that the State should become a "demonic" force.[23] In the New Testament it is not suggested that by its very nature, as it were, the State will be compelled, sooner or later, to play the part

[23] Political events of the last decades have introduced into New Testament exegesis on this matter a certain pessimism which seems to me not to be justified by the actual facts of the case. The State of Revelation 13 is, as H. Schlier (*Die Beurteilung des Staates,* op. cit., p. 329) rightly maintains, "the borderline of the possible State."

of "the Beast out of the abyss." Why should this be inevitable, since it, too, has been created in Christ, through
Him and for Him, and since even to it the manifold wisdom
of God is proclaimed by the Church? It could not itself
become a Church, but from its very origin, in its concrete
encounter with Christ and His Church, it could administer
justice and protect the law (in accordance with its substance, dignity, function, and purpose, and in so doing remaining true to itself instead of losing itself!). In so doing,
voluntarily or involuntarily, very indirectly yet none the less
certainly, it would be granting the gospel of justification a
free and assured course. In the light of the New Testament
doctrine of angels, it is impossible to ignore the fact that
the State may also manifest its neutral attitude towards
Truth, by rendering to the Church, as a true and just State,
that service which lies in its power to render; by granting
it its true and lawful freedom, "that we may lead a quiet
and peaceable life in all godliness and honesty" (I Timothy
2:2). If, even when it has become an unjust State and a
persecutor of the Church, it cannot escape the real subordination in which it exists, yet in the same real subordination it may also show its true face as a just State (in practice, that may well mean at least a part of its true face)
as, indeed, it appears to have manifested it to a great extent in all that concerns Paul, according to the Acts of the
Apostles.[24]

Thus there is clearly no cause for the Church to act as
though it lived, in relation to the State, in a night in which
all cats are grey. It is much more a question of continual
decisions, and therefore of distinctions between one State

[24] Up to the present, the κατέχον and κατέχων of II Thessalonians 2:6 ff. have been taken to indicate that function of the
Roman State which works against the Antichrist. Had this
interpretation not been "unfortunately" shattered by O. Cullmann, this passage would also have to be considered here. (*Le
caractère eschatologique du devoir missionaire et de la conscience
apostolique de St. Paul.* Recherches théologiques, Strasbourg,
1936, pp. 26–61.)

and another, between the State of yesterday and the State of to-day. According to I Corinthians 12:10 the Church receives, among other gifts, that of "discerning of spirits." If by these "spirits" we are to understand the angelic powers, then they have a most significant political relevance in preaching, in teaching, and in pastoral work.

One decisive result of this exegesis as a whole should be a clear understanding of the meaning of Romans 13. The God from Whom all this concrete authority comes, by Whom all powers that be are ordained (v. 1), Whose ordinance every man resists who resists that power (v. 2), Whose διάκονος it is (v. 4), and Whose λειτουργοί its representatives are (v. 6)—this God cannot be understood apart from the Person and the Work of Christ; He cannot be understood in a general way as Creator and Ruler, as was done in the expositions of the Reformers, and also by the more recent expositors up to and including Dehn and Schlier. When the New Testament speaks of the State, we are, fundamentally, in the *Christological* sphere; we are on a lower level than when it speaks of the Church, yet, in true accordance with its statements on the Church, we are in the same unique Christological sphere. It is not sufficient to state[25] that the ὑπὸ θεοῦ sweeps away all hypotheses which suggest that the origin of the State is in nature, in fate, in history, or in a social contract of some kind, or in the nature of society, and the like; this, too, is why it is not sufficient to state that the foundation of the State reminds it of its limits. The phrase ὑπὸ θεοῦ does mean this, it is true, but it must be added that in thus stating this foundation and limitation of the State, Paul is not thinking of some general conception of God, in the air, so to speak, but he is indicating Him in Whom all the angelic powers have their foundation and their limits, the "image of the invisible God" Who as such is also "the first-born of all creation" (Colossians 1:15). We need only see

25 With H. Schlier, *Die Beurteilung des Staates,* op. cit., p. 323.

that for Paul, within the compass of *this* centre and therefore *within* the Christological sphere (although outside the
sphere characterized by the word "justification"), there was
embodied in the angelic world another secondary Christological sphere—if I may put it so—uniting the Church with
the Cosmos, wherein the necessity and the reality of the
establishment and administration of human justice were
clearly important above all else—thus we need only see this
in order to note that in Romans 13 the Name of God is
used in a very clear way, and not in any vague manner.
The establishment and the function of the State, and, above
all, the Christian's attitude towards it, will then lose a certain accidental character which was peculiar to the older
form of exposition. We shall then not have to relate to God,
as distinct from Jesus Christ, the grounds for the attitude
required by I Peter 2:13, "for the Lord's sake"[26]; just as in
the use of similar formulae in the epistles to the Colossians
and the Ephesians, according to the specific witness of Colossians 3:24 and Ephesians 5:20; 6:6, no other "Lord" is
meant than Jesus Christ. "Submitting yourselves one to another in the fear of *Christ*" (Ephesians 5:21, R. V.). It is
the fear of Christ—that is, the sense of indebtedness to Him
as the Lord of all created lords (Colossians 4:1; Ephesians
6:9) which would be dishonoured by an attitude of hos-
tility, and it is the fear of Christ which clearly, according
to I Peter 2:13 f., forms the foundation for the imperative:
"Submit yourselves . . . to the King." And we shall have
to think in the same direction when in Romans 13:5 it is
claimed of the same submission that it should occur not
merely through anxiety before the wrath of authority but
for conscience' sake. Συνείδησις (conscience) means
"to know with." With *whom* can man *know something?*
The New Testament makes this quite clear. Schlatter has
translated the συνείδησις θεοῦ of I Peter 2:19 as "certainty
of God." It is clear that in I Corinthians 10:25-27, where the

[26] With G. Dehn, op. cit., p. 99.

formula used in Romans 13:5 also appears, it does not indicate a norm imposed upon mankind in general but one imposed on the Christian in particular—and that from the recognition of that norm implies that he must adopt a definite attitude. Christian knowledge, Christian certainty, and the Christian conscience do not demand that Christians should enquire in the shambles or at the feast about the origin of the meat that is set before them (I Corinthians 10). But the Christian conscience does demand that they should submit to authority (Romans 13). Clearly this is because in this authority we are dealing indirectly, but in reality, with the authority of Jesus Christ.

III. THE SIGNIFICANCE OF THE STATE
FOR THE CHURCH

In order to throw light upon the contrast between Church and State emphasis has always, rightly, been laid on the fact that the State (πολίτευμα) or the city (πόλις) of Christians should not be sought in the "present age" but in that "which is to come"; not on earth but in heaven. That is, in an impressive way, the theme of Philippians 3:20; Hebrews 11:10, 13–16; 12:22; 13:14. And in Revelation 21 this city of the Christians is surveyed and presented, with its walls, gates, streets, and foundations: "The holy city, new Jerusalem, coming down from God out of heaven, prepared as a bride adorned for her husband" (v. 2). In this city there is, strikingly, no temple: "For the Lord God the Almighty, and the Lamb, are the temple thereof" (v. 22). That is why it is said: "The nations shall walk in the light of it: and the kings of the earth do bring their glory and honour into it. And the gates of it shall not be shut at all by day: (for there shall be no night there). And they shall bring the glory and honour of the nations into it. And there shall in no wise enter into it anything that defileth, neither whatsoever worketh abomination or maketh a lie; but they which are written in the Lamb's book of life" (v. 24–27). It must here be emphasized, above all else, that in this future city in which Christians have their citizenship here and now (without yet being able to inhabit it), we are concerned not with an ideal but with a real State—yes, with the only real State; not with an imaginary one but with the only one that truly exists. And it is the fact that Christians have their citizenship in this, the real State, that makes them strangers and sojourners within the State, or within the States of this age and this world. Yes, if they are "strangers and pilgrims" here it is because this city constitutes below their faith and their hope—and not because they see the imperfections or even the perversions of the states of this age and this world! It is not resentment, but a positive sentiment, through which, in contradistinction to non-Christians, it comes about, that they have "no continuing city" here (Hebrews 13:14). It is because Paul knows that he is "garrisoned" by the Peace of God which passes all understanding, that the *Pax Romana* cannot impress Paul as an "ultimate."[27] It is because "the saints shall judge the world"—and not because the Corinthian law-courts were particularly bad—that, according to I Corinthians 6:1–6, Christians must be able, within certain limits, to renounce their right to appeal to the law of the State and its courts of justice.

It is the hope of the new age, which is dawning in power, that separates the Church from the State, that is, from the States of this age and this world. The only question is whether this same hope does not also in a peculiar way unite the two. H. Schlier,[28] who rightly answers the question in the affirmative, describes this bond as follows: "Whoever considers human life as ordered and established in faith, for this world which God is preparing . . . in face of the claims of the actual earthly bonds, and in the claims of the most exacting of all bonds—that of the State—will discern in them the will of God, and will see bonds estab-

---

[27] Cf. K. L. Schmidt, *Theologische Blätter*, 1937, No. 1, p. 8.
[28] *Die Beurteilung des Staates*, op. cit., p. 320.

lished by God. In the eschatological knowledge about the actual end of the world, the present world is proclaimed in its real and true character as the creation of God's word." To that I would like to ask whether the New Testament anywhere shows any interest in the "present world in its real and true character as the creation of God" save in so far as it finds it to be grounded, constituted, and restored in Christ? In this case, when we think of this bond, should we not do better to look forward, to the coming age, to Christ? rather than backward—that is, rather than think in the abstract about creation and the hypothetic divine bonds established by this creation.

Of one thing in the New Testament there can be no doubt: namely, that the description of the order of the new age is that of a *political* order. Think of the significant phrase: the Kingdom of God, or of Heaven, that it is called *Kingdom* of God or Heaven, and remember, too, the equally "political" title of the King of this realm: *Messias* and *Kyrios*. And from Revelation 21 we learn that it is not the real church (ἐκκλησία) but the real city (πόλις) that truly constitutes the new age. Or, to put it otherwise, the Church sees its future and its hope, not in any heavenly image of its own existence but in the real heavenly *State*. Wherever it believes in, and proclaims here and now, the justification of the sinner through the blood of the Lamb, it will see before it, "coming down out of Heaven from God," the city of eternal *law* in which there is no offender and whose doors need never be closed, but which also needs no temple, for the same Lamb will be its temple. And this city will not endure merely on the ruins of the annihilated glory of the peoples and the kings of this earth, but the whole of this earthly glory will be brought into it, as supplementary tribute. Could the Church of divine justification hold the human law-State in higher esteem than when it sees in that very State, in its heavenly reality, into which its terrestrial existence will finally be absorbed, the final predicate of its own grounds for hope? Deification of the

124

State then becomes impossible, not because there is no divinity of the State, but because it is the divinity of the *heavenly* Jerusalem, and as such cannot belong to the *earthly* State. But the opposite of such deification, which would consist of making the State a devil, is also impossible. We have no right to do as Augustine liked to do, and straightway identify the *civitas terrena* with the *civitas Cain*. Not because its representatives, office-bearers, and citizens can protect it from becoming the State of Cain, or even of the devil, but because the heavenly Jerusalem is also a State, and every State, even the worst and most perverse, possesses its imperishable destiny in the fact that it will one day contribute to the glory of the heavenly Jerusalem, and will inevitably bring its tribute thither.

From this point of view we can understand two passages from the Epistle to the Ephesians, in which the writer—although the word of the Kingdom of God which is not of this world was known to him, if not in those actual words, at least in reality—has no hesitation in describing the Church itself (in a connection in which he is considering its earthly and temporal reality) as the commonwealth of Israel (Ephesians 2:12) and later describes its members (in contradistinction to their past nature as strangers and foreigners) as fellow-citizens with the saints (Ephesians 2:19). There is no need to labour the point that this "politicizing" of the earthly Church is "from above," affirmed from the point of view of the ultimate reality, of the "last things," which, however, neither removes nor alters the fact that in this age, and in relation to the State, the Church is a "stranger." But, for that very reason, it is remarkable that the concepts, so important for the Christians, of "strangers and foreigners" are used to describe those who do not belong to the Church, and that the concept of the "rights of citizenship," so important for the ancient State, can become the predicate of the Church on earth. Here, too, we must ask whether the objection of the early Christians to the earthly State, and the consciousness of being "strangers" within this

State, does not mean essentially that this State has been too little (and not too much!) of a State for those who know of the true State in heaven; or, again, we might put the question positively, and ask whether, in view of the basis and origin of the earthly State, these Christians have not seen, in the Gospel of divine justification, the infinitely better, the true and only real source and norm of all human law, even in this "present age." The desire or the counsel of Paul, in I Corinthians 6:1–6, which so clearly points to something like legislation within the Church itself would otherwise be incomprehensible.

It is essential that we should arrive at this point—one might almost say at this prophecy: that it is the preaching of justification of the Kingdom of God, which founds, here and now, the true system of law, the true State. But it is equally essential that when this prophecy has been made, the Church on earth should not go beyond its own bounds and endow itself with the predicates of the heavenly State, setting itself up in concrete fashion against the earthly State as the true State. That it could and should do so cannot possibly be the meaning of Ephesians 2 and I Corinthians 6, because for the New Testament the *heavenly* State is and remains exclusively the *heavenly* State, established not by man but by God, which, as such, is not capable of realization in this age, not even in the Church. It was from the point of view of a later age that Clement of Alexandria[29] extolled the Church guided by the Logos as unconquered, enslaved by no arbitrary power, and even identical with the will of God on earth as in heaven; and again, later still, Augustine[30] was able to make the proud statement: "True justice is not to be found except in that republic, whose founder and ruler is Christ." It could be no accident that the writers of the Epistle to the Hebrews and the First Epistle of Peter neglected to console the Christians who were so homeless in this age and in this world by assuring

[29] *Strom.* IV., 171, 2.
[30] *De civ. Dei* II., 21.

them that nevertheless they had a home, here and now, in the Church. It is far more true that they have here *no* abiding city, and that the earthly Church stands over against the earthly State as a sojourning (παροικία) and not as a State within the State, or even as a State above the State, as was later claimed by the papal Church of Rome, and widened also by many a fanatical sect.

There are other conclusions to be drawn from Ephesians 2 and I Corinthians 6. This παροικία, this "establishment among strangers," does not wait for the city which is to come without doing anything. What indeed does take place in this παροικία? We might reply, simplifying, but not giving a wrong turn to the phrase: the preaching of justification. It is in this preaching that this "foreign community" affirms its hope in the city which is to come: in this preaching, that is, in the message which proclaims that by grace, and once for all, God has gathered up sinful man in the Person of Jesus, that He has made sin and death His own, and thus that He has not merely acquitted man, but that for time and for eternity He has set him free for the enjoyment of the life which he had lost. What the παροικία believes is simply the reality of this message, and what it hopes for is simply the unveiling of this reality, which still remains, here and now, concealed. We must note that it is not man or humanity, but the Lamb, the Messiah, Jesus, who is the Spouse for whom the Bride, the heavenly city, is adorned. It is He, and His Presence, as "the Lamb that hath been slain," who makes this City what it is, the City of Eternal Law. It is *His* law, the rights won by Jesus Christ in His death and proclaimed in His Resurrection which constitute this Eternal law. (Here we are confronted by a quite different conception from the Stoic conception of the "City" to which Clement of Alexandria refers in the passage which we have mentioned.) Now this eternal law of Jesus Christ constitutes precisely the content of the message of justification, in which, here and now, the task of the Church consists. The Church cannot itself effect the disclosure of this

eternal law, neither in its own members nor in the world.
It cannot anticipate the "Marriage of the Lamb" (Revelation 19:7). It cannot will to celebrate it in this "present
age" but it can and it should proclaim it.

But—here we go a step further—it can and should proclaim it to the world. It is worth noticing that in all those
passages in the Epistles that are directly concerned with
our problem a window is thrown open in this direction,
which, at first sight, seems somewhat strange. The behaviour towards the State which they demand from all Christians is always connected with their behaviour towards *all*
men. "Render therefore to all their dues. . . . Owe *no man*
anything but (which you can only do within the Church)
to love one another" (Romans 13:7, 8). In I Timothy 2:1
we read that they should make "supplications, prayers, intercessions and giving of thanks for *all* men," and in Titus
3:2, immediately after the words on those in authority, we
read "be gentle, showing all meekness unto *all* men." Finally in I Peter 2:13 we are again dealing with the "*Every*
ordinance of man," and later in verse 17, going a step further (and here too in clear distinction to the love of the
brotherhood) "honour all men." What does this mean? It
seems to me, when considered in connection with I Timothy
2:1–7, that it clearly means this: since it is our duty to
pray for all men, so we should pray in particular for kings
and for all in authority, because it is only on the condition
that such men exist that we can "lead a quiet and peaceable
life in all godliness and honesty." Why is it necessary that
we should be able to lead such a life? Are we justified[31]
in interpolating at this point the words "as citizens," and
so causing Christians to pray for the preservation of a sort
of bucolic existence? The passage quite clearly goes on to
say: "For this (obviously the possibility of our quiet and
peaceable life) is good and acceptable in the sight of God
our Saviour, who will have all men to be saved, and to come

[31] With H. Schlier, *Die Beurteilung des Staates*, op. cit., p. 325.

unto the knowledge of the truth. For there is *one* God, and *one* mediator between God and men, the man Christ Jesus; who gave Himself a ransom for all, to be testified in due time. Whereunto I am ordained a preacher and an apostle." Thus the quiet and peaceable life under the rule of the State, for the sake of which this passage calls us to pray for statesmen, is no ideal in itself, just as the existence of the Church, in contradistinction to all other men, can be no ideal in itself. It is the preacher and apostle who stands in need of this quiet and peaceable life, and this apostle, and with him stand those with whom he here identifies himself, not in the service of a Universal Creator and Preserver, but in the service of the Saviour, God, who will "have all men to be saved and to come unto the knowledge of the truth," who is the one God in the one Mediator, who gave Himself a ransom for all. Why does the community need "a quiet and peaceable life"? It needs it because in its own way, and in its own place, it likewise needs the preacher and apostle for all, and because it needs freedom in the realm of all men in order to exercise its function towards all men. But this freedom can only be guaranteed to it through the existence of the earthly State which ordains that all men shall live together in concord. Is not the argument for submission to the civil administration of justice given in I Peter 2:15 f., by the statement that it is the will of God that the Christians, as those who are recognized by law as well-doers, "may put to silence the ignorance of foolish men—as free and not using their liberty" guaranteed by the State "for a cloak of maliciousness," but will act in this freedom as servants of God? Since this freedom of the Church can only be guaranteed through the existence of the State, therefore there is no alternative but that the Church should on its side guarantee the existence of the State through its prayers. That this mutual guarantee can and should fundamentally be only temporary—that is, that by its very nature it can and should be exercised only in this age and in this world, that the State can and should only partially grant or totally deny the guarantee that the Church demands of it, that, finally, the Church cannot and should not require of the State any guarantee as to the validity or the effectiveness of its gospel—all this is not the least altered by the fact that the Church in all earnestness expects this *limited* guarantee from the State, nor by the fact that this guarantee which the Church requires of the State is a serious one and, as such, cannot be too seriously laid upon the hearts of its members. Prayer for the bearers of State authority belongs to the very essence of its own existence. It would not be a Church if it were to ignore this apostolic exhortation. It would then have forgotten that it has to proclaim this promised justification to *all* men.

But we must also understand the demand for loyalty to the State in the other passages in the epistles which deal with this subject in the light of I Timothy 2, that is, in the light of this mutual guarantee. In Titus 3:1–8, astonishingly enough, it is connected with the rebirth through baptism and the Holy Spirit. But that is not astonishing if the future heirs of eternal life, justified, according to verse 7, by the grace of Jesus Christ, receive all that not for themselves, but in the Church and as members of the Church for *all* men, and thus stand in need of freedom not for themselves but for the word of the Church and therefore for human law, and so have to respect the bearers and representatives of that law. And when, in Romans 13:3–4 and I Peter 2:14, we read that obedience must be rendered to authority because it is the duty of authority to reward the good and to punish the evil, then in the context of both epistles it seems to me an impossible interpretation to say that the writers were speaking of "good" and "evil" in a quite general and neutral sense, and that the justice of the State is equally general and neutral. Why should not the writers have been making the same use of these concepts as they did elsewhere and been demanding that Christians should do the good work of their faith, in the performance of which they, in contradistinction to the evildoers, have

130

in no sense to fear the power of the State, but rather to expect its praise? Why, thinking of the "power" that was so clearly granted to Pilate to crucify or release Jesus, should they not first of all have pointed Christians to the better— i.e., the only true—possibility of the State, the possibility granted to it by the "good," i.e., by the Church, to protect the law (or, in other words, the possibility of a "Concordat"!)? The fact that the State could actually make use of the other possibility, that it could actually honour the evil and punish the good, may be quite true, but it cannot alter its mission, hence it does not affect the Christian attitude towards the State. Should the State go so far as to honour evildoers and to punish the good, if it can be recalled at all to its mission, and thereby to its own true possibility, it will be due to the Christian attitude towards it. And even if the State betrays its divine calling, it will nevertheless be constrained to fulfil its function, to guarantee the freedom of the Church, even if in a quite different way! The "honour" that the State owes to the Church will then consist in the suffering of the followers of Christ, described in the First Epistle of Peter:—and the punishment of the evildoers will then consist in the fact that the glory of this suffering will be withheld from them. Thus in one way or another the State will have to be the servant of divine justification.

Thus it is clear that in this very close relation between the existence of the Church and that of the State, the Church cannot itself become a State, and the State, on the other hand, cannot become a Church. It is true, of course, that in principle the Church, too, turns to all men; but it does so with its message of justification and its summons to faith. The Church gathers its members through free individual decisions, behind which stands the quite different free choice of God, and in this age it will never have to reckon with gathering all men within itself. The Church must have complete confidence in God, who is the God of *all* men, and must leave all to Him. But the State has always assembled within itself all men living within its boundaries, and it holds them together, as such, through its order, which is established and maintained by force. The State as State knows nothing of the Spirit, nothing of love, nothing of forgiveness. The State bears the sword, and at the best, as seen in Romans 13, it does not wield it in vain. It, too, must leave to God the question of what must be done for man's welfare, in addition to the administration of the law which is based on force. The State would be denying its own existence if it wished to become a Church. And the Church on its side, for its own sake, or rather, for the sake of its mission, can never wish that the State should cease to be the State. For it can never become a true Church. If it were insane enough to attempt this, it could only become an idolatrous Church. And, on the other hand, the Church would be denying its own existence if it wished to become a State and to establish law by force, when it should be preaching justification. It could not be a true State; it could only be a clerical State, with a bad conscience on account of its neglected duty, and incapable, on this foreign soil, of administering justice to all men, as is the duty of the State.

But this relation between the Church and the State does not exclude—but includes—the fact that the *problem* of the State, namely, the problem of law, is raised, and must be answered, within the sphere of the Church on Earth. Those phrases in Ephesians 2 are no mere rhetorical flourishes, but they are concretely related to the fact that there is and must be within the Church itself (and here its close relation to the State asserts itself) *something like* (I am here deliberately using an indefinite phrase) a commonwealth: with its offices and orders, divisions of labour and forms of community. This is known as *Ecclesiastical Law*. It is well known that Rudolf Sohm regarded the appearance of ecclesiastical law (which, according to him, took place only in the second century) as the great sin of the early Church. But the Christian Church of the first century, as pictured by Sohm, moved freely by the Spirit of God, hither and thither, never actually existed. Now there is *one* fundamental ecclesiastical principle which cannot be denied without at the same time denying the resurrection of Christ and, in so doing, the very heart of the entire New Testament: the authority of the apostolate. And from the start there arose from this one principle many others, in freedom indeed, but in the freedom of the Word of God, and in no other freedom. The words of Paul (I Corinthians 14:33) about the God who is the author not of confusion but of peace, and above all the whole argument of I Corinthians 12–14, are characteristic at this point. How could the Church expect law from the State and at the same time exclude law from its own life? How could it, and how can it, live out the teaching with which it has been entrusted and yet, in its own realm, dispense with law and order, with the order which serves to protect that teaching? Certainly, in the primitive Church there was not more than "something like a commonwealth"; it was certainly never a juridical community employing the methods of compulsion characteristic of the State; and when, later on, it became such a body it was to its own undoing. Ecclesiastical authority is spiritual authority—authority, that is, which implies the witness of the Holy Spirit. Does this make it less strict? Is it not for that very reason the strictest authority of all? Was there ever a more compelling legal order than that which we find presupposed in the letters of the Apostles?

But the other side of the question, in this connection, is still more remarkable: this antagonistic relation between Church and State does not exclude—on the contrary, it includes—the fact that the New Testament, if we examine it closely, in no sense deals with the order of the State, and the respect that is due to such an order, as something which affects the life of the Christian community only from without, but to *a certain extent* (and again I am deliberately using an indefinite phrase) the New Testament deals with it as the question of a kind of annexe and outpost of the

Christian community, erected in the world outside, which thus, in a certain sense, is included within the ecclesiastical order as such. The fact that the Church has had to assume a "certain" political character is balanced by the fact that the Church must recognize, and honour, a "certain" ecclesiastical character in the State. At all times, indeed, forms of "State Church" have always existed, which, in this respect at least, were not so far removed from the New Testament picture of things as might appear at first glance. It should be noted that the exhortation on the subject of the State in Romans 13 cannot possibly, if taken in its context, be regarded as an exceptional statement dealing with the Law of Nature, because it is firmly embedded in the midst of a series of instructions all of which have as their presupposition and their aim the Christian existence as such. In the First Epistle to Timothy it stands at the head of a series of exhortations dealing with the conduct of men and of women during worship, and with the office of the bishop and of the deacon. In the Epistle to Titus it stands at the end, and in the First Epistle of Peter at the beginning, of a similar series. The verb "be subject unto," so characteristic of the imperative of this exhortation (Romans 13:1; Titus 3:1; I Peter 2:13), is used not only in Titus 2:9 and I Peter 2:18 for the conduct of Christian slaves towards their masters but also in Colossians 3:18, Ephesians 5:22, Titus 2:5, and I Peter 3:1, 5 for the conduct of women towards men, in I Peter 5:5 for the conduct of the younger towards the older members of the community, and in Ephesians 5:21 and I Peter 5:5 for the conduct of Christians towards one another within the Church.

How do the "higher powers," the "rulers," the king and his governors come into this society? Does not the fact that they are within this society clearly show that this is a specifically *Christian* exhortation, that the secular authority and our attitude to it are to some extent included in those "orders" in which Christians have to prove their obedience to God? and indeed to the God who is revealed in Jesus

Christ? And what shall we say to the fact that the State ruler in Romans 13:4 is characterized as the minister of God, and the State officials in Romans 13:6, with their various demands on the public, as God's ministers?[32] How do they come to receive this sacred name? It seems to me clear that they do "to a certain extent" actually stand within the sacred order, not—as was later said, with far too great a servility—as *membra prœcipua,* but as *ministri extraordinarii ecclesiœ.*

The light which falls from the heavenly polis upon the earthly *ecclesia* is reflected in the light which illuminates the earthly polis from the earthly *ecclesia,* through their mutual relation. If the question of how this mutual relation can be explained is not actually answered by I Timothy 2 coupled with Revelation 21, then a better explanation would have to be found. But in any case, as such, the phenomenon cannot well be denied.

IV. THE SERVICE WHICH THE CHURCH OWES
TO THE STATE

If we review the New Testament exhortations to Christians on the subject of their relation to the State, we are certainly justified in placing intercession (I Timothy 2) in a central position, as being the most intimate of all, and the one which includes all others. But we must be careful to see just how all-inclusive this particular exhortation is. Christians are called to offer "supplications, prayers, intercessions and thanksgivings" for all men, and in particular for kings and all who are in positions of authority. Does the passage actually say less than this: that the Church has (not as one incidental function among others, but in the whole essence of its existence as a Church) to offer it-

---

[32] In Romans 15:16 and Philippians 2:25, Paul describes himself and his fellow worker Epaphroditus as λειτουργὸν Ἰησοῦ χριστοῦ εἰς τὰ ἔθνη; in Hebrews 1:2 the name is given to the angels of God and in Hebrews 8:2 to Christ Himself!

self to God for all men, and in particular for the bearers of State power? But this "offering oneself for" all men means (for that is the significance of the ὑπέρ) that the Church is fulfilling, on its side, that worship of God which men cannot and will not accomplish, yet which must be accomplished. This intercession is necessary because from God alone can rulers receive and maintain that power which is so salutary for the Church and, for the sake of the preaching of justification, so indispensable to all men. Far from being the *object* of worship, the State and its representatives need prayer *on their behalf*. In principle, and speaking comprehensively, this is the essential service which the Church owes to the State. This service includes all others. In so doing, could the Church more clearly remind the State of its limits? or more clearly remind itself of its own freedom? than in thus offering itself on its behalf?

But this service must of course be rendered without asking whether the corresponding service owed by the State to the Church is also being given, and indeed without inquiring whether the individual bearers of State power are worthy of it. How could such inquiry be made before rendering a service of this kind? Clearly the service becomes all the more necessary the more negative the answer to the question; just as the nature of justification comes out still more clearly when we see that he who is "justified" is evidently a real and thorough sinner in the sight of God and man. Thus the more negative the answer to this question, the more urgently necessary is the priestly duty laid upon the Church; the most brutally unjust State cannot lessen the Church's responsibility for the State; indeed, it can only increase it.

Our understanding of "Be in subjection. . . ." in Romans 13:1 f. and the other passages would have been better served if we had not regarded this particular exhortation in the abstract, but had considered it in its relationship to this first, primary exhortation. Can this "subjection," fundamentally, mean anything other than the practical behaviour on the part of the members of the Church which corresponds to the priestly attitude of the Church as such? "Be subject unto" (ὑποτασσεδθαί) does not mean directly and absolutely "to be subject to someone," but to respect him as his office demands. We are here dealing with a subjection that is determined and conditioned by the framework within which it takes place, namely, by a definite τάξις (order). But the τάξις (as in other passages in which the word occurs) is not set up by the persons concerned who are to be the objects of respect, but, according to verse 2, it is based on the ordinance of God. It is on the basis, then, of this divine ordinance that such respect must be shown. But in what way can this due respect be shown to the leaders of the State, unless Christians behave towards it in the attitude of mind which always expects the best from it—expects, that is, that it will grant legal protection to the free preaching of justification—but which is also prepared—under certain circumstances—to carry this preaching into practice by suffering injustice instead of receiving justice, and thereby acknowledging the State's power to be, in one way or another, God-given? If Christians were not to do this, if they were to oppose this ordinance and thus to refuse the State authority the respect which is determined and limited by divine decree, then, according to verse 2, they would be opposing the will of God, and their existence within the sphere of the State would become their condemnation. If they neither reckoned with this positive divine claim of the State nor were prepared, if need be, to suffer injustice at its hands, then by that very fact they would belong to those evil ones who must fear its power, and towards whom, by the use of its sword and the power of compulsion that is granted to it, it could only, openly or secretly ("power as such is evil"), be the force which executes the divine wrath, the dread manifestation of the perdition of this age (verses 4–5).

But this respect for the authority of the State which is demanded in Romans 13 must not be separated—in theory or in practice—from the priestly function of the Church. It cannot possibly consist of an attitude of abstract and absolute elasticity towards the intentions and undertakings of the State, simply because, according not only to the Apocalypse but also to Paul, the possibility may arise that the power of the State, on its side, may become guilty of opposition to the Lord of lords, to that divine ordinance to which it owes its power. If Christians are still to respect the State, even then, their docility in this instance can only be passive and, as such, limited. The "subjection" can in no case mean that the Church and its members will approve, and wish of their own free will to further, the claims and undertakings of the State, if once the State power is turned not to the protection but to the suppression of the preaching of justification. Even then, Christians will never fail to grant that which is indispensable to the State power as guardian of the public law, as an ordained power— "tribute to whom tribute is due, custom to whom custom, fear to whom fear, honour to whom (as representative and bearer of ἐξουσία) honour—even if the State abuses this ἐξουσία and demonstrates its opposition, as a demonic power, to the Lord of lords. Even then, according to Matthew 22:21, Christians will render unto Caesar the things which are Caesar's, i.e., whatever is his due, not as a good or a bad Caesar, but simply as Caesar; the right which is his, even if he turns that right to wrong. As has been shown, it is and remains a God-established ἐξουσία, and that which we owe it, even then, must not be withheld. But the fact also remains, unalterably, that Christians are to render unto God the things which are God's; and likewise, that the Church must be and must remain the Church. Thus the "subjection" required of Christians can *not* mean that they accept and take upon themselves responsibility for those intentions and undertakings of the State which directly or indirectly are aimed against the freedom of preaching. Of course it must be understood that even then the "subjection" will not cease. But their submission, their

respect for the power of the State to which they continue
to give what they owe, will consist in becoming its victims,
who, in their concrete action will not accept any responsibility, who cannot inwardly co-operate, and who as "subjects" will be unable to conceal the fact, and indeed ought
to express it publicly, in order that the preaching of justification may be continued under all circumstances. All this
will be done, not *against* the State, but as the Church's
service *for* the State! Respect for the authority of the State
is indeed an annexe to the priestly function of the Church
towards the State. Christians would be neglecting the distinctive service which they can and must render to the
State, were they to adopt an attitude of unquestioning as-
sent to the will and action of the State which is directly
or indirectly aimed at the suppression of the freedom of the
Word of God. For the possibility of intercession for the
State stands or falls within the freedom of God's Word.
Christians would, in point of fact, become enemies of any
State if, when the state threatens their freedom, they did
not resist, or if they concealed their resistance—although
this resistance would be very calm and dignified. Jesus
would, in actual fact, have been an enemy of the State if
He had *not* dared, quite calmly, to call King Herod a "fox"
(Luke 13:32). If the State has perverted its God-given authority, it cannot be honoured better than by this *criticism*
which is due to it in all circumstances. For this power that
has been perverted, what greater service can we render
than that of intercession? Who can render this service better than the Christian? And how could Christians intercede,
if, by themselves acquiescing in the perversion of the power
of the State, they had become traitors to their own cause?
And where would be their respect for the State if it involved such betrayal?

Through this discussion of the "subjection" of Romans
13:1 (in its connection with I Timothy 2:1), we have
gained a fundamental insight into the nature of the service
which the Church, as the organ of divine justification, owes

to the State, as the organ of human law, which the State has a right to expect from it, and by which, if it remains obedient, it can actually assist the State. We have affirmed that there is a mutual guarantee between the two realms. We now ask: what is the guarantee which the Church has to offer to the State?

After all that we have seen as constituting the relation between the two realms, the answer must be given: that apart from the Church, nowhere is there any fundamental knowledge of the reasons which make the State legitimate and necessary. For everywhere else, save in the Church, the State, and every individual state, with its concern for human justice, may be called in question. From the point of view of the Church that preaches divine justification to all men this is impossible. For in the view of the Church, the authority of the State is included in the authority of their Lord Jesus Christ. The Church lives in expectation of the eternal State, and therefore honours the earthly State, and constantly expects the best from it, i.e., that, in its own way amongst "all men," it will serve the Lord whom the believers already love as their Saviour. For the sake of the freedom to preach justification, the Church expects that the State will be a true State, and thus that it will create and administer justice. But the Church honours the State even when this expectation is not fulfilled. It is then defending the State against the State, and by rendering unto God the things that are God's, by obeying God rather than man, through its intercession it represents the only possibility of restoring the State and of saving it from ruin. States may rise and fall, political conceptions may change, politics as such may interest or may fail to interest men, but throughout all developments and all changes *one* factor remains, as the preservation and basis of all states—the Christian Church. What do statesmen and politicians themselves know of the authorization and the necessity of their function? Who or what can give them the assurance that this function of theirs is not, as such, an illusion, however seriously they may take it? And further, what do those others know, whose responsibility for the State and its law the statesman alone can represent, and on whose co-operation they are finally so dependent! Just as divine justification is the continuum of law, so the Church is the political continuum. And to be this is the Church's first and fundamental service to the State. The Church need only be truly "Church," and it will inevitably render this service. And the State receives this service, and secretly lives by it, whether it knows and gratefully acknowledges it or not, whether it wishes to receive it or not.

We only *seem* to be moving in a lower sphere when, turning again to Romans 13:5-7, we note that the Church here demands from her members, with an insistence elsewhere unparalleled, the fulfilment of those *duties* on the performance of which not merely the goodness or the badness of the State but its very existence as a State depends. The fact that the right to impose rates and taxes belongs to the State, that its laws and their representatives should be honoured, as such, with all respect and reverence, can only be stated unreservedly and in a binding way from the standpoint of the divine justification of sinful man, because this provides the only protection against the sophisms and excuses of man, who is always so ready to justify himself and is always secretly trying to escape from true law. The Church knows that the State can neither establish nor protect true human law, *"ius unum et necessarium,"* that is, the law of freedom for the preaching of justification, unless it receives its due from the Church, whereby alone it can exist as guarantor of law—that is why the Church demands that this due should be rendered in all circumstances.

We would of course give a great deal to receive more specific instruction in Romans 13—and elsewhere in the New Testament—about what is and what is not to be understood by these particular political duties towards the State which are expected of the Church. The questions which arise in this connection cannot be answered directly from the New Testament; all that we can do is to give replies which are derived from the consideration of these passages by carrying the thought further along the same lines.

Could Romans 13:7, for instance, also mean "an oath to whom an oath"? Does the rendering of an oath, if demanded by the State, belong to those duties that must be fulfilled? The Reformers, as we know, answered this question in the affirmative, but on looking at Matthew 5:33 ff., we could wish that they had given a little more thought to the matter. So much, at least, is certain, even if the question is answered in the affirmative, that an oath to the State *cannot* be given (with true respect for the State!) if it is a "totalitarian" oath (that is, if it is rendered to a name which actually claims Divine functions). Such an oath would indeed imply that those who swear it place themselves at the disposition of a power which threatens the freedom of the Word of God; for Christians, therefore, this would mean the betrayal of the Church and of its Lord.

Again, is *military service* one of these self-evident duties to the State? The Reformers again answered this question in the affirmative, and again we could wish that they had done so with a little more reserve. Because the State "beareth the sword" (Romans 13), it is clear that it participates in the murderous nature of the present age. Yet on this matter, at least in principle, we cannot come to a conclusion which differs from that of the Reformers. Human law needs the guarantee of human force. Man would not be a sinner in need of justification if it were otherwise. The State that is threatened from within or without by force needs to be prepared to meet force by force, if it is to continue to be a state. The Christian must have very real grounds for distrusting the State if he is to be entitled to refuse the State his service, and if the Church as such is to be entitled and called to say "No" at this point. A fundamental Christian "No" cannot be given here, because it would in fact be a fundamental "No" to the earthly State as such, which is impossible from the Christian point of view. And here I should like to add, in relation to the question of national defense in Switzerland in particular, that here, too, there can for us be no practical refusal of military service. We may have grave misgivings about the way in which the Swiss State seeks to be a just state, but, all the same, we cannot maintain that it confronts the Church like "the Beast out of the abyss" of Revelation 13. But this may and should be said of more than one other State to-day, against which it is worthwhile to defend our own legal administration. And since this is the case, from the Christian point of view we are right in seeking to defend our frontiers; and if the State in Switzerland takes steps to organize this security (it is not inconceivable that the Church should give its support to the State in this matter), we cannot close our eyes to the question of how far the Church in Switzerland should stand in all surety behind the State.[33]

It is quite another question whether the State has any right to try to strengthen its authority by making any kind of *inward* claim upon its subjects and its citizens; that is, whether it has any right to demand from them a particular philosophy of life (Weltanschauung), or at least sentiments and reactions dominated by a particular view imposed by the State from without. According to the New Testament, the only answer to this question is an unhesitating "No"! Claims of this kind can in no way be inferred from Romans 13; they have no legal justification whatsoever. On the contrary, here we are very near the menace of "the Beast out of the abyss"; a just State will not require to make such claims. From Romans 13 it is quite clear that love is not one of the duties which we owe to the State. When the State begins to claim "love," it is in process of becoming a Church, the Church of a false God, and thus an unjust State. The just State requires, not love, but a simple, resolute, and responsible attitude on the part of its citizens. It

[33] It is obvious that the same is also true of the Church in Czechoslovakia, in Holland, in Denmark, in Scandinavia, in France and, above all, in England.

is this attitude which the Church, based on justification, commends to its members.

Far more difficult, because far more fundamental, is another apparent gap in the teaching of the New Testament. It lies in the fact that the New Testament seems to speak concretely only of a purely authoritarian State, and so to speak of Christians only as subjects, not as citizens who, in their own persons, bear some responsibility for the State. But it is to be hoped that the fulfilment of our political duty is not exhausted by the payment of taxes and other such passive forms of legality. For us the fulfilment of political duty means rather responsible choice of authority, responsible decision about the validity of laws, responsible care for their maintenance, in a word, political action, which may and must also mean political struggle. If the Church were not to guarantee the modern State the fulfilment of such duties, what would it have to offer the "democratic" State? Here, too, we must ask: are we following a legitimate line of expansion of the thought of Romans 13? It may seem audacious to answer that question in the affirmative, yet it must be firmly answered in the affirmative. Everything here depends on whether we are justified in this connection in taking the "be subject unto" of Romans 13 together with the exhortation to intercession in I Timothy 2. If the prayer of Christians for the State constitutes the norm of their "subjection," which would only be an "annexe" of the priestly function of the Church, and if this prayer is taken seriously as the responsible intercession of the Christians for the State, then the scheme of purely passive subjection which apparently—but only apparently—governs the thought of Romans 13 is broken. Then the serious question arises: is it an accident that in the course of time "democratic" States have come into being, States, that is, which are based upon the responsible activity of their citizens?[34]

[34] Under this category it is proper to include also such "monarchies" as those of England and Holland. The assertion that all forms of government are equally compatible or incompatible

Can serious prayer, in the long run, continue without the corresponding work? Can we ask God for something which we are not at the same moment determined and prepared to bring about, so far as it lies within the bounds of our possibility? Can we pray that the State shall preserve us, and that it may continue to do so as a just State, or that it will again become a just State, and not at the same time pledge ourselves personally, both in thought and action, in order that this may happen, without sharing the earnest desire of the Scottish Confession[35] and saying, with it: *"Vitae bonorum adesse, tyrranidem opprimere, ab infirmioribus vim improborum defendere,"* thus without, in certain cases, like Zwingli,[36] reckoning with the possibility of revolution, the possibility, according to his strong expression, that we may have to "overthrow with God" those rulers who do not follow the lines laid down by Christ? Can we give the State that respect which is its due without making its business our own, with *all* the consequences that this implies? When I consider the deepest and most central content of the New Testament exhortation, I should say that we are justified, from the point of view of exegesis, in regarding the "democratic conception of the State" as a justifiable expansion of the thought of the New Testament. This does not mean that the separation between justification and justice, between Church and State, the fact that Christians are "foreigners" in the sphere of the State, has been abolished. On the contrary, the resolute intention of the teaching of the New Testament is brought out still more plainly when it is clear that Christians must not only endure the earthly State but that they must *will* it, and that they can-

---

with the Gospel is not only outworn but false. It is true that a man may go to hell in a democracy and achieve salvation under a mobocracy or a dictatorship. But it is not true that a Christian can endorse, desire, or seek after a mobocracy or a dictatorship as readily as a democracy.

[35] Art. 14.
[36] Schlussreden, Art. 42.

not will it as a "Pilate" State, but as a *just* State; when it is seen that there is no outward escape from the political sphere; when it is seen that Christians, while they remain within the Church and are wholly committed to the future "city," are equally committed to responsibility for the earthly "city," called to work and (it may be) to struggle, as well as to pray, for it; in short, when each one of them is responsible for the character of the State as a just State. And the democratic State might as well recognize that it can expect no truer or more complete fulfilment of duty than that of the citizens of the realm that is so foreign to it as a State—the Church founded on divine justification.

There is one last point to be discussed concerning the guarantee that the Church has to grant to the State. We remember how the New Testament exhortation to a certain extent culminates in the affirmation that Christians should render unto Caesar the things that are Caesar's by their well-doing. But what does this mean if by this "well-doing" we understand not a neutral moral goodness, but a life lived in faith in Jesus Christ, the life of the Children of God, the life of the Church as such? It then means that the essential service of the Church to the State simply consists in maintaining and occupying its own realm as Church. In so doing it will secure, in the best possible way, the position of the State, which is quite different. By proclaiming divine justification it will be rendering the best possible assistance to the establishment and maintenance of human justice and law. No direct action that the Church might take (acting partly or wholly politically, with well-meaning zeal) could even remotely be compared with the positive relevance of that action whereby, without any interference with the sphere of the State, this Church proclaims the coming Kingdom of Christ, and thereby the gospel of justification through faith alone; I mean that its action consists in true scriptural *preaching*, and *teaching*, and in the true and scriptural administration of the *sacraments*. When it performs this action the Church is, within the order of creation, the force which founds and maintains the State. If the State is wise, in the last resort it will expect and demand from the Church nothing other than this, for this includes everything that the Church can render to the State, even all the political obligations of its members. And we can and may formulate the matter even more precisely: the guarantee of the State by the Church is finally accomplished when the Church claims for itself the guarantee of the State, i.e., the guarantee of freedom to proclaim her message. This may sound strange, but this is the case: all that can be said from the standpoint of divine justification on the question (and the questions) of human law is summed up in this one statement: the Church *must have freedom to proclaim divine justification.* The State will realize its own potentialities, and thus will be a just State, in proportion as it not merely positively allows, but actively grants, this freedom to the Church; i.e., in proportion as it honourably and consistently desires to be the State within whose realm (whether as national Church or otherwise is a secondary question) the Church exists which has this freedom as its right. We know that the earthly State is neither called, nor able, to establish on earth the eternal law of the heavenly Jerusalem, because no human beings are either called, or able, to perform that task. But the State is called to establish human law, and it has the capacity to do so. We cannot measure what this law is by any Romantic or Liberalistic idea of "natural law," but simply by the concrete law of freedom, which the Church must claim for its Word, so far as it is the Word of God. This right of the Church to liberty means the foundation, the maintenance, the restoration of everything—certainly of all human law. Wherever this right is recognized, and wherever a true Church makes the right use of it (and the free preaching of justification will see to it that things fall into their true place), there we shall find a legitimate human authority and an equally legitimate human independence; tyranny on the one hand, and anarchy on the other, Fascism and Bolshevism alike, will be dethroned; and the true order of human affairs—the justice, wisdom and peace, equity and care for human welfare which are necessary to that true order—will arise. Not as heaven (not even as a miniature heaven) on earth! No, this "true order" will be able to arise only upon this *earth* and within the *present age,* but this will take place *really* and *truly,* already upon this earth, and in this present age, in this world of sin and sinners. No eternal Solomon, free from temptation and without sin, but none the less a Solomon, an image of Him whose Kingdom will be a Kingdom of Peace without frontiers and without end. This is what the Church has to offer to the State when, on its side, it desires from the State nothing but freedom. What more could the State require, and what could be of greater service to it than this—to be taken so inexorably seriously?

We all know the maxim of Frederick the Great: *Suum cuique.* It is a less well-known fact that it already appears as a definition of human law, as a summary of the functions of the just State, in Calvin's *Institutio: ut suum cuique salvum sit et incolume.*[37] But—this Calvin did not say, and this we must attempt to discover and to learn anew—it depends upon the justification of sinful man in Jesus Christ, and thus on the maintenance of this central message of the Christian Church, that all *this* should become true and valid in every sense, in the midst of this "world that passeth away," in the midst of the great, but temporary contrast between Church and State, in the period which the Divine patience has granted us between the resurrection of Jesus Christ and His return: *Suum cuique.*

[37] Inst. IV., 20, 3. And, as was kindly pointed out to me by Dr. Arnold Eberhard of Lörrach, there is no doubt that Calvin was on his side quoting Ulpian and Cicero.

THE CHRISTIAN
COMMUNITY AND THE
CIVIL COMMUNITY

I

By the "Christian community" we mean what is usually
called "the Church" and by the "civil community" what is
usually called "the State."

The use of the concept of the "community" to describe
both entities may serve at the very outset to underline the
positive relationship and connexion between them. It was
probably with some such intention in mind that Augustine
spoke of the *civitas coelestis* and *terrena* and Zwingli of divine and human justice. In addition, however, the twofold
use of the concept "community" is intended to draw attention to the fact that we are concerned in the "Church" and
the "State" not merely and not primarily with institutions
and offices but with human beings gathered together in cor-
porate bodies in the service of common tasks. To interpret
the "Church" as meaning above all a "community" has
rightly become more recognised and normal again in recent
years. The Swiss term "civil community"—in Swiss villages
the residential, civil, and ecclesiastical communities often
confer one after the other in the same inn, and most of the
people involved belong to all three groups—the "civil community" as opposed to the "Christian community" may also
remind Christians that there are and always have been

communities outside their own circle in the form of States, i.e. political communities.

The "Christian community" (the Church) is the commonalty of the people in one place, region, or country who are called apart and gathered together as "Christians" by reason of their knowledge of and belief in Jesus Christ. The meaning and purpose of this "assembly" (*ekklesia*) is the common life of these people in one Spirit, the Holy Spirit, that is, in obedience to the Word of God in Jesus Christ, which they have all heard and are all needing and eager to hear again. They have also come together in order to pass on the Word to others. The inward expression of their life as a Christian community is the one faith, love, and hope by which they are all moved and sustained; its outward expression is the Confession by which they all stand, their jointly acknowledged and exercised responsibility for the preaching of the Name of Jesus Christ to all men and the worship and thanksgiving which they offer together. Since this is its concern, every single Christian community is as such an ecumenical (catholic) fellowship, that is, at one with the Christian communities in all other places, regions, and lands.

The "civil community" (the State) is the commonalty of all the people in one place, region, or country in so far as they belong together under a constitutional system of government that is equally valid for and binding on them all, and which is defended and maintained by force. The meaning and purpose of this mutual association (that is, of the *polis*) is the safeguarding of both the external, relative, and provisional freedom of the individuals and the external and relative peace of their community and to that extent the safeguarding of the external, relative, and provisional humanity of their life both as individuals and as a community. The three essential forms in which this safeguarding takes place are (a) legislation, which has to settle the legal system which is to be binding on all; (b) the government and administration which has to apply the legislation; (c) the

administration of justice which has to deal with cases of
doubtful or conflicting law and decide on its applicability.

II

When we compare the Christian community with the
civil community the first difference that strikes us is that in
the civil community Christians are no longer gathered together as such but are associated with non-Christians (or
doubtful Christians). The civil community embraces everyone living within its area. Its members share no common
awareness of their relationship to God, and such an awareness cannot be an element in the legal system established
by the civil community. No appeal can be made to the
Word or Spirit of God in the running of its affairs. The civil
community as such is spiritually blind and ignorant. It has
neither faith nor love nor hope. It has no creed and no
gospel. Prayer is not part of its life, and its members are not
brothers and sisters. As members of the civil community
they can only ask, as Pilate asked: What is truth? Since
every answer to the question abolishes the presuppositions
of the very existence of the civil community. "Tolerance"
is its ultimate wisdom in the "religious" sphere—"religion"
being used in this context to describe the purpose of the
Christian community. For this reason the civil community
can only have external, relative, and provisional tasks and
aims, and that is why it is burdened and defaced by something which the Christian community can, characteristi-
cally, do without: physical force, the "secular arm" which
it can use to enforce its authority. That is why it lacks the
ecumenical breadth and freedom that are so essential to
Christianity. The *polis* has walls. Up till now, at least, civil
communities have always been more or less clearly marked
off from one another as local, regional, national, and therefore competing and colliding units of government. And that
is why the State has no safeguard or corrective against the
danger of either neglecting or absolutising itself and its par-

ticular system and thus in one way or the other destroying and annulling itself. One cannot in fact compare the Church with the State without realising how much weaker, poorer, and more exposed to danger the human community is in the State than in the Church.

III

It would be inadvisable, however, to make too much of the comparison. According to the fifth thesis of the *Theological Declaration* of Barmen (1934), the Christian community also exists in "the still unredeemed world," and there is not a single problem harassing the State by which the Church is not also affected in some way or other. From a distance it is impossible clearly to distinguish the Christian from the non-Christian, the real Christian from the doubtful Christian even in the Church itself. Did not Judas the traitor participate in the Last Supper? Awareness of God is one thing, Being in God quite another. The Word and Spirit of God are no more automatically available in the Church than they are in the State. The faith of the Church can become frigid and empty; its love can grow cold; its hope can fall to the ground; its message become timid and even silent; its worship and thanksgiving mere formalities; its fellowship may droop and decay.

Even the Church does not simply "have" faith or love or hope. There are dead churches, and unfortunately one does not have to look far to find them anywhere. And if, normally, the Church renounces the use of physical force and has not shed blood, sometimes the only reason has been lack of opportunity; struggles for power have never been entirely absent in the life of the Church. Again, side by side with other and more far-reaching centrifugal factors, local, regional, and national differences in the Church's way of life have been and still are strong. The centripetal forces which it needs are still weak enough to make even the unity of Christian communities among themselves extremely doubtful in many places and a special "ecumenical" movement both desirable and urgently necessary. There is then no cause for the Church to regard the civil community too superciliously.

IV

More important still, however, is the positive relationship between the two communities which results from the fact that the constitutive elements of the civil community are also proper and indispensable to the Christian community. The very term *ekklesia* is borrowed from the political sphere. The Christian community also lives and acts within the framework of an order of law which is binding on all its members, of a "canon law" which it cannot regard as an end in itself but which it cannot neglect to institute as a "token of the Lordship of Christ" (A. de Quervain, *Kirche, Volk und Staat,* 1945, p. 158). The Christian community exists at all times and places as a *politeia* with definite authorities and offices, with patterns of community life and divisions of labour. What the legislature, the executive, and the administration of the law are in the life of the State has its clear parallels in the life of the Church, however freely and flexibly it may be shaped and however "spiritually" it may be established and intended. And though the Christian community does not embrace all men, but only those who profess themselves Christians and would like, more or less seriously, to be Christians—it reaches out, instituted as it is to be the "light of the world," from these few or many, to all men. The gospel, with which it is commissioned, is preached to all, applies to all. To serve all the people within range of the place, region, or country where it is established is the purpose of its existence no less than it is that of the civil community. In I Timothy 2:1–7 we read that the God in whose sight it is good and acceptable that Christians as such may lead a quiet and peaceable life in all godliness and honesty will have all men to be saved and to come to the knowledge of the truth, and that Christians are therefore to pray for all men and especially for "kings," that is, for those who bear special responsibility in the political sphere (which embraces all men).

In this sense, therefore, the existence of the Christian community is political. Furthermore, the object of the promise and the hope in which the Christian community has its eternal goal consists, according to the unmistakable assertion of the New Testament, not in an eternal Church but in the *polis* built by God and coming down from heaven to earth, and the nations shall walk in the light of it and the kings of the earth will bring their glory and honour into it (Revelation 21:2, 24)—it consists in a heavenly *politeuma* (Philippians 3:20)—in the *basileia* of God—in the judgment of the King on the throne of His glory (Matthew 25:31 f.). Bearing all this in mind, we are entitled and compelled to regard the existence of the Christian community as of ultimate and supremely political significance.

V

The Christian community is particularly conscious of the need for the existence of the civil community. For it knows that all men (non-Christians as well as Christians) need to have "kings," that is, need to be subject to an external, relative, and provisional order of law, defended by superior authority and force. It knows that the original and final pattern of this order is the eternal Kingdom of God and the eternal righteousness of His grace. It preaches the Kingdom of God in this external form. But it also thanks God that His Kingdom has an external, relative, and provisional embodiment "in the world that is not yet redeemed," in which it is valid and effective even when the temporal order is based on the most imperfect and clouded knowledge of Jesus Christ or on no such knowledge at all. This external, relative, and provisional, but not on that account invalid or ineffective, form of legal order is the civil community. The Christian community is aware of the need for the civil community, and it alone takes the need absolutely seriously. For—because it knows of the Kingdom and grace of God—it knows of man's presumption and the plainly destructive consequences of man's presumption. It knows how dangerous man is and how endangered by himself. It knows him as a sinner, that is as a being who is always on the point of opening the sluices through which, if he were not checked in time, chaos and nothingness would break in and bring human time to an end. It can only conceive the time that is still left to it as a "time of grace" in the twofold sense of being the time which it is given in order to know and lay hold of God's grace—and as the time which it is given for this very purpose by the grace of God. The Christian community itself exists in this time which is given to man, that is, in the space where man's temporal life is still protected from chaos—and on the face of it chaos should have broken in long ago. It sees as the visible means of this protection of human life from chaos the existence of the civil community, the State's effort to achieve an external, relative, and provisional humanising of man's life and the political order instituted for all (for non-Christians as well as Christians—they both need it, for human arrogance is alive in both), under which the evil are punished and the good rewarded (Romans 13:3; I Peter 2:14) and which guarantees that the worst is prevented from happening. It knows that without this political order there would be no Christian order. It knows and it thanks God that—as the inner circle within the wider circle (cf. O. Cullmann, *Königscherrschaft Christi und Kirche im Neuen Testament*, 1941)—it is allowed to share the protection which the civil community affords.

VI

Knowing that, it recognises in the existence of the civil community—disregarding the Christianity or lack of Christianity of its members and officials and also disregarding the particular forms which it assumes—no less than in its own existence, the operation of a divine ordinance (*ordinatio*, i.e. institution or foundation), an *exousia* which is and acts in accordance with the will of God (Romans 13:1 f.). However much human error and human tyranny may be involved in it, the State is not a product of sin but one of the constants of the divine Providence and government of the world in its action against human sin: it is therefore an instrument of divine grace. The civil community shares both a common origin and a common centre with the Christian community. It is an order of divine grace inasmuch as in relation to sinful man as such, in relation to the world that still needs redeeming, the grace of God is always the patience of God. It is the sign that mankind, in its total ignorance and darkness, which is still, or has again become, a prey to sin and therefore subject to the wrath of God, is yet not forsaken but preserved and sustained by God. It serves to protect man from the invasion of chaos and therefore to give him time: time for the preaching of the gospel; time for repentance; time for faith. Since "according to the measure of human insight and human capacity" and "under the threat and exercise of force" (Barmen Thesis No. 5), provision is made in the State for the establishment of human law and (in the inevitably external, relative, and provisional sense) for freedom, peace, and humanity, it renders a definite service to the divine Providence and plan of salvation, quite apart from the judgment and individual desires of its members. Its existence is not separate from the Kingdom of Jesus Christ; its foundations and its influence are not autonomous. It is outside the Church but not outside the range of Christ's dominion—it is an exponent of His Kingdom. It is, according to the New Testament, one of the "powers" created through Him and in Him and which subsist in Him (Colossians 1:16 f.), which cannot separate us from the love of God (Romans 8:37 f.) because they are all given to Him and are at His disposal (Matthew 28:18).

The activity of the State is, as the Apostle explicitly stated (Romans 13:4, 6), a form of divine service. As such it can be perverted just as the divine service of the Church itself is not exempt from the possibility of perversion. The State can assume the face and character of Pilate. Even then, however, it still acts in the power which God has given it ("Thou couldest have no power at all against me, except it were given thee from above": John 19:11). Even in its perversion it cannot escape from God; and His law is the standard by which it is judged. The Christian community therefore acknowledges "the benefaction of this ordinance of His with thankful, reverent hearts" (Barmen Thesis No. 5). The benefaction which it acknowledges consists in the external, relative, and provisional sanctification of the unhallowed world which is brought about by the existence of political power and order. In what concrete attitudes to particular political patterns and realities this Christian acknowledgement will be expressed can remain a completely open question. It makes one thing quite impossible, however: a Christian decision to be indifferent; a non-political Christianity. The Church can in no case be indifferent or neutral towards this manifestation of an order so clearly related to its own mission. Such indifference would be equivalent to the opposition of which it is said in Romans 13:2 that it is a rebellion against the ordinance of God—and rebels secure their own condemnation.

VII

The Church must remain the Church. It must remain the inner circle of the Kingdom of Christ. The Christian community has a task of which the civil community can never relieve it and which it can never pursue in the forms peculiar to the civil community. It would not redound to the welfare of the civil community if the Christian community were to be absorbed by it (as Rothe has suggested that it should) and were therefore to neglect the special task which it has received a categorical order to undertake. It proclaims the rule of Jesus Christ and the hope of the Kingdom of God. This is not the task of the civil community; it has no message to deliver; it is dependent on a message being delivered to it. It is not in a position to appeal to the authority and grace of God; it is dependent on this happening elsewhere. It does not pray; it depends on others praying for it. It is blind to the whence and whither of human existence; its task is rather to provide for the external and provisional delimitation and protection of human life; it depends on the existence of seeing eyes elsewhere. It cannot call the human *hybris* into question fundamentally, and it knows of no final defence against the chaos which threatens it from that quarter; in this respect, too, it depends on ultimate words and insights existing elsewhere. The thought and speech of the civil community waver necessarily between a much too childlike optimism and a much too peevish pessimism in regard to man—as a matter of course it expects the best of everybody and suspects the worst! It obviously relies on its own view of man being fundamentally superseded elsewhere. Only an act of supreme disobedience on the part of Christians could bring the special existence of the Christian community to an end. Such a cessation is also impossible because then the voice of what is ultimately the only hope and help which all men need to hear would be silent.

VIII

The Christian community shares in the task of the civil community precisely to the extent that it fulfils its own task. By believing in Jesus Christ and preaching Jesus Christ it believes in and preaches Him who is Lord of the world as He is Lord of the Church. And since they belong to the inner circle, the members of the Church are also automatically members of the wider circle. They cannot halt at the boundary where the inner and outer circles meet, though the work of faith, love, and hope which they are under orders to perform will assume different forms on either side of the boundary. In the sphere of the civil community the Christian community shares common interests with the world and its task is to give resolute practical expression to this community of interest. The Christian community prays for the civil community. It does so all the more since the civil community as such is not in the habit of praying. But by praying for it, it also makes itself responsible for it before God, and it would not be taking this responsibility seriously if it did no more than pray, if it did not also work actively on behalf of the civil community. It also expresses its active support of the civil community by acknowledging that, as an operation of a divine ordinance, the civil power is also binding on Christians and significant and just from the Christian point of view. It expresses its active support of the civil community by "subordinating" itself, in the words of the Apostle (Romans 13:1), to the cause of the civil community under all circumstances (and therefore whatever the political form and reality it has to deal with *in concreto*). Luther's translation speaks of "being *subject*" (cf. English A.V.: "Let every soul be *subject* to the higher powers"—Trans.), which is something dangerously different from what is meant here. The last thing this instruction implies is that the Christian community and the Christian should offer the blindest possible obedience to the civil community and its officials. What is meant is (Romans 13:6 f.) that Christians should carry out what is required of them for the establishment, preservation, and maintenance of the civil community and for the execution of its task, because, although they are Christians and, as such, have their home elsewhere, they also live in this outer circle. Jesus Christ is still its centre: they, too, are therefore responsible for its stability. "Subordination" means the carrying out of this joint responsibility in which Christians apply themselves to the same task with non-Christians and submit themselves to the same rule. The subordination accrues to the good of the civil community however well or however badly that community is defended, because the civil cause (and not merely the Christian cause) is also the cause of the one God. In Romans 13:5 Paul has expressly added that this "subordination" is not optional but necessary, and necessary not merely "for fear of punishment," for fear of the otherwise inevitable conflict with an obscure commandment of God, but "for conscience sake": in the clear evangelical knowledge of the divine grace and patience, which is also manifested in the existence of the State and, therefore, in full responsibility towards the will of God which the Christian sees revealed in the civil community. The "subordination" will be an expression of the obedience of a free heart which the Christian offers to God in the civil sphere as in the sphere of the Church—although with a different purpose (he renders to Caesar what is Caesar's and to God what is God's—Matthew 22:21).

IX

In making itself jointly responsible for the civil community, the Christian community has no exclusive theory of its own to advocate in face of the various forms and realities of political life. It is not in a position to establish one particular doctrine as *the* Christian doctrine of the just State. It is also not in a position to refer to any past realisation of the perfect State or to hold out any prospect of one in the future. There is but one Body of Christ, born of the Word of God, which is heard in faith. There is therefore no such thing as a Christian State corresponding to the Christian Church; there is no duplicate of the Church in the political sphere. For if, as the effect of a divine ordinance, as the manifestation of one of the constants of divine Providence and of the historical process which it governs, the State is in the Kingdom of Christ, this does not mean that God is revealed, believed, and perceived in any political community as such. The effect of the divine ordinance is that men are entrusted (whether or not they believe it to be a divine revelation) to provide "according to the measure of human insight and human capacity" for temporal law and temporal peace, for an external, relative, and provisional humanisation of man's existence. Accordingly, the various political forms and systems are human inventions which as such do not bear the distinctive mark of revelation and are not witnessed to as such—and can therefore not lay any claim to belief. By making itself jointly responsible for the civil community, the Christian community participates—on the basis of and by belief in the divine revelation—in the human search for the best form, for the most fitting system of political organisation; but it is also aware of the limits of all the political forms and systems which man can discover (even with the co-operation of the Church), and it will beware of playing off one political concept—even the "democratic" concept—as *the* Christian concept, against all others. Since it proclaims the Kingdom of God it has to maintain its own hopes and questions in the face of all purely political concepts. And this applies even more to all political achievements. Though the Christian will be both more lenient and more stern, more patient and more impatient towards them than the non-Christian, he will not regard any such achievement as perfect or mistake it for the Kingdom of God—for it can only have been brought about by human insight and human ability. In the face of all political achievements, past, present, and future, the Church waits for "the city which hath foundations, whose builder and maker is God" (Hebrews 11:10). It trusts and obeys no political system or reality but the power of the Word, by which God upholds all things (Hebrews 1:3; Barmen Thesis No. 5), including all political things.

X

In this freedom, however, the Church makes itself responsible for the shape and reality of the civil community in a quite definite sense. We have already said that it is quite impossible for the Christian to adopt an attitude of complete indifference to politics. But neither can the Church be indifferent to particular political patterns and realities. The Church "reminds the world of God's Kingdom, God's commandment and righteousness and thereby of the responsibility of governments and governed" (Barmen Thesis No. 5). This means that the Christian community and the individual Christian can understand and accept many things in the political sphere—and if necessary suffer and endure everything. But the fact that it can understand much and endure everything has nothing to do with the "subordination" which is required of it, that is, with the share of responsibility which it is enjoined to take in the political sphere. That responsibility refers rather to the decisions which it must make before God: "must" make, because, unlike Christian understanding and suffering, Christian intentions and decisions are bound to run in a quite definite direction of their own. There will always be room and need for discussion on the details of Christian intentions and decisions, but the general line on which they are based can never be the subject of accommodation and compromise in the Church's relations with the world. The Christian community "subordinates" itself to the civil community by making its knowledge of the Lord who is Lord of all its criterion, and distinguishing between the just and the unjust State, that is, between the better and the worse political form and reality; between order and caprice; between government and tyranny; between freedom and anarchy; between community and collectivism; between personal rights and individualism; between the State as described in Romans 13 and the State as described in Revelation 13. And it will judge all matters concerned with the establishment, preservation, and enforcement of political order in accordance with these necessary distinctions and according to the merits of the particular case and situation to which they refer. On the basis of the judgment which it has formed it will choose and desire whichever seems to be the better political system in any particular situation, and in accordance with this choice and desire it will offer its support here and its resistance there. It is in the making of such distinctions, judgments, and choices from its own centre, and in the practical decisions which necessarily flow from that centre, that the Christian community expresses its "subordination" to the civil community and fulfils its share of political responsibility.

XI

The Christian decisions which have to be made in the political sphere have no idea, system, or programme to refer to but a direction and a line that must be recognised and adhered to in all circumstances. This line cannot be defined by appealing to the so-called "natural law." To base its policy on "natural law" would mean that the Christian community was adopting the ways of the civil community, which does not take its bearings from the Christian centre and is still living or again living in a state of ignorance. The Christian community would be adopting the methods, in other words, of the pagan State. It would not be acting as a Christian community in the State at all; it would no longer be the salt and the light of the wider circle of which Christ is the centre. It would not only be declaring its solidarity with the civil community: it would be putting itself on a par with it and withholding from it the very things it lacks most. It would certainly not be doing it any service in that way. For the thing the civil community lacks (in its neutrality towards the Word and Spirit of God) is a firmer and clearer motivation for political decisions than the so-called natural law can provide. By "natural law" we mean the embodiment of what man is alleged to regard as universally right and wrong, as necessary, permissible, and forbidden "by nature," that is, on any conceivable premise. It has been connected with a natural revelation of God, that is, with a revelation known to man by natural means. And the civil community as such—the civil community which is not yet or is no longer illuminated from its centre —undoubtedly has no other choice but to think, speak, and act on the basis of this allegedly natural law, or rather of a particular conception of the court of appeal which is passed off as *the* natural law. The civil community is reduced to guessing or to accepting some powerful assertion of this or that interpretation of natural law. All it can do is to grope around and experiment with the convictions which it derives from "natural law," never certain whether it may not in the end be an illusion to rely on it as the final authority and therefore always making vigorous use, openly or secretly, of a more or less refined positivism. The results of the politics based on such considerations were and are just what might be expected. And if they were and are not clearly and generally negative, if in the political sphere the better stands alongside the worse, if there were and still are good as well as bad States—no doubt the reality is always a curious mixture of the two!—then the reason is not that the true "natural law" has been discovered, but simply the fact that even the ignorant, neutral, pagan civil community is still in the Kingdom of Christ, and that all political questions and all political efforts as such are founded on the gracious ordinance of God by which man is preserved and his sin and crime confined.

What we glimpse in the better kind of State is the purpose, meaning, and goal of this divine ordinance. It is operative in any case, even though the citizens of the particular State may lack any certain knowledge of the trustworthy standards of political decision, and the overwhelming threat of mistaking an error for the truth may be close at hand. The divine ordinance may operate with the co-operation of the men and women involved, but certainly without their having deserved it: *Dei providentia hominum confusione.* If the Christian community were to base its political responsibility on the assumption that it was also interested in the problem of natural law and that it was attempting to base its decisions on so-called natural law, this would not alter the power which God has to make good come of evil, as He is in fact always doing in the political order. But it would mean that the Christian community was sharing human illusions and confusions. It is bad enough that, when it does not risk going its own way, the Christian community is widely involved in these illusions and confusions. It should not wantonly attempt to deepen such involvement. And it would be doing no less if it were to seek the criterion of its political decisions in some form of the so-called natural law. The tasks and problems which the Christian community is called to share, in fulfilment of its political responsibility, are "natural," secular, profane tasks and problems. But the norm by which it should be guided is anything but natural: it is the only norm which it can believe in and accept as a spiritual norm, and is derived from the clear law of its own faith, not from the obscure workings of a system outside itself: it is from knowledge of this norm that it will make its decisions in the political sphere.

XII

It is this reliance on a spiritual norm that makes the Christian community free to support the cause of the civil community honestly and calmly. In the political sphere the Church will not be fighting for itself and its own concerns. Its own position, influence, and power in the State are not the goal which will determine the trend of its political decisions. "My Kingdom is not of this world. If my Kingdom were of this world, then would my servants fight that I should not be delivered to the Jews, but now is my Kingdom not from hence" (John 18:36). The secret contempt which a Church fighting for its own interests with political weapons usually incurs even when it achieves a certain amount of success is well deserved. And sooner or later the struggle generally ends in mortifying defeats of one sort or another. The Christian community is not an end in itself. It serves God and it thereby serves man. It is true that the deepest, ultimate, divine purpose of the civil community consists in creating opportunities for the preaching and hearing of the Word and, to that extent, for the existence of the Church. But the only way the State can create such opportunities, according to the providence and ordinance of God, is the natural, secular, and profane way of the establishment of law, the safeguarding of freedom and peace, "according to the measure of human insight and capacity." The divine purpose is therefore not at all that the State should itself gradually develop more or less into a Church. And the Church's political aim cannot be to turn the State into a Church, that is, make it as far as possible subservient to the tasks of the Church. If the State grants the Church freedom, respect, and special privileges in any of the ways which are open to it (guarantees of one kind or another, a share in education and broadcasting, the defence of the Sabbath, financial reliefs or subsidies, and the like), the Church will not immediately start dreaming of a Church-State. It will be thankful for the State's help, seeing in such help a result of the divine providence and ordinance: and it will show its gratitude by being a Church all the more faithfully and zealously within the broader frontiers that the State's gifts make possible, thereby justifying the expectation which the State evidently reposes in it. But it will not claim such gifts as a right. If they are refused, it will look in itself for the reason, not in the State. "Resist not evil!" is an injunction that applies here. The Church will ask itself whether it has already given proof to the State of the Spirit and the power of God, whether it has already defended and proclaimed Jesus Christ to the world to the extent that it can expect to be considered an important, significant, and salutary factor in public life. It will ask, for example, whether it is in a position to say the tremendous things that are certainly entitled to be heard in schools. It will first and foremost do penance—when and where would it not have cause for so doing?—and it will do that best by concentrating on its own special work in the, possibly, extremely small space left to it in public life, with all the more confidence and intensity and with redoubled zeal, "with the greatest force applied at the narrowest point." Where it has first to advertise its desire to play a part in public life, where it must first establish its claim to be considered a factor of public importance, it only proves that its claim to be heard is irrelevant and it thoroughly deserves not to be heard at all, or to be heard in a way that will sooner or later afford it no pleasure. Whenever the Church has entered the political arena to fight for its claim to be given public recognition, it has always been a Church which has failed to understand the special purpose of the State, an impenitent, spiritually unfree Church.

XIII

The Church cannot, however, simply take the Kingdom of God itself into the political arena. The Church reminds men of God's Kingdom. This does not mean that it expects the State gradually to become the Kingdom of God. The Kingdom of God is the Kingdom where God is without shadow, without problems and contradictions, where He is All in All: it is the rule of God in the redeemed world. In the Kingdom of God the outward is annulled by the inward, the relative by the absolute, the provisional by the final. In the Kingdom of God there is no legislature, no executive, no legal administration. For in the Kingdom of God there is no sin to be reproved, no chaos to be feared and checked. The Kingdom of God is the world dominion of Jesus Christ in honour of the Father, revealed in the clear light of day. The State as such, the neutral, pagan, ignorant State knows nothing of the Kingdom of God. It knows at best of the various ideals based on natural law. The Christian community within the State does know about the Kingdom of God, however, and it brings it to man's attention. It reminds men of the Jesus Christ who came and is to come again. But it cannot do this by projecting, proposing, and attempting to enforce a State in the likeness of the Kingdom of God. The State is quite justified if it refuses to countenance all such Christian demands. It belongs to the very nature of the State that it is not and cannot become the Kingdom of God. It is based on an ordinance of God which is intended for the "world not yet redeemed" in which sin and the danger of chaos have to be taken into account with the utmost serious-ness and in which the rule of Jesus Christ, though in fact already established, is still hidden. The State would be dis-avowing its own purpose if it were to act as though its task was to become the Kingdom of God. And the Church that tried to induce it to develop into the Kingdom of God could be rightly reproached for being much too rashly presump-tuous. If its demand were to have any meaning at all, it would have to believe that its own duty was also to develop into the Kingdom of God. But, like the State, the Church also stands "in the world not yet redeemed." And even at its best the Church is not an image of the Kingdom of God. It would appear that when it makes this demand on the State, the Church has also confused the Kingdom of God with a mere ideal of the natural law. Such a Church needs to be reminded again of the real Kingdom of God, which will follow both State and Church in time. A free Church will not allow itself to be caught on this path.

XIV

The direction of Christian judgments, purposes, and ideals in political affairs is based on the analogical capaci-ties and needs of political organisation. Political organisation can be neither a repetition of the Church nor an anticipa-tion of the Kingdom of God. In relation to the Church it is an independent reality; in relation to the Kingdom of God it is (like the Church itself) a human reality bearing the stamp of this fleeting world. An equating of State and

Church on the one hand and State and Kingdom of God on the other is therefore out of the question. On the other hand, however, since the State is based on a particular divine ordinance, since it belongs to the Kingdom of God, it has no autonomy, no independence over against the Church and the Kingdom of God. A simple and absolute heterogeneity between State and Church on the one hand and State and Kingdom of God on the other is therefore just as much out of the question as a simple and absolute equating. The only possibility that remains—and it suggests itself compellingly—is to regard the existence of the State as an allegory, as a correspondence and an analogue to the Kingdom of God which the Church preaches and believes in. Since the State forms the outer circle, within which the Church, with the mystery of its faith and gospel, is the inner circle, since it shares a common centre with the Church, it is inevitable that, although its presuppositions and its tasks are its own and different, it is nevertheless capable of reflecting indirectly the truth and reality which constitute the Christian community. Since, however, the peculiarity and difference of its presuppositions and tasks and its existence as an outer circle must remain as they are, its justice and even its very existence as a reflected image of the Christian truth and reality cannot be given once and for all and as a matter of course but are, on the contrary, exposed to the utmost danger; it will always be questionable whether and how far it will fulfil its just purposes. To be saved from degeneration and decay it needs to be reminded of the righteousness which is a reflection of Christian truth. Again and again it needs a historical setting whose goal and content are the moulding of the State into an allegory of the Kingdom of God and the fulfilment of its righteousness. Human initiative in such situations cannot proceed from the State itself. As a purely civil community, the State is ignorant of the mystery of the Kingdom of God, the mystery of its own centre, and it is indifferent to the faith and gospel of the Christian community. As a civil community it can only draw from the porous wells of the so-called natural law. It cannot remind itself of the true criterion of its own right-eousness, it cannot move towards the fulfilment of that righteousness in its own strength. It needs the wholesomely disturbing presence, the activity that revolves directly around the common centre, the participation of the Christian community in the execution of political responsibility. The Church is not the Kingdom of God, but it has knowledge of it; it hopes for it; it believes in it; it prays in the name of Jesus Christ, and it preaches His Name as the Name above all others. The Church is not neutral on this ground, and it is therefore not powerless. If it achieves only the great and necessary *metabasis eis allo genos* which is the share of political responsibility which it is enjoined to assume, then it will not be able to be neutral and powerless and deny its Lord in the other *genos*. If the Church takes up its share of political responsibility, it must mean that it is taking that human initiative which the State cannot take: it is giving the State the impulse which it cannot give itself; it is reminding the State of those things of which it is unable to remind itself. The distinctions, judgments, and choices which it makes in the political sphere are always intended to foster the illumination of the State's connexion with the order of divine salvation and grace and to discourage all the attempts to hide this connexion. Among the political possibilities open at any particular moment it will choose those which most suggest a correspondence to, an analogy and a reflection of, the content of its own faith and gospel.

In the decisions of the State, the Church will always support the side which clarifies rather than obscures the Lordship of Jesus Christ over the whole, which includes this political sphere outside the Church. The Church desires that the shape and reality of the State in this fleeting world should point towards the Kingdom of God, not away from it. Its desire is not that human politics should cross the politics of God, but that they should proceed, however distantly, on parallel lines.

It desires that the active grace of God, as revealed from heaven, should be reflected in the earthly material of the external, relative, and provisional actions and modes of action of the political community. It therefore makes itself responsible in the first and last place to God—the one God whose grace is revealed in Jesus Christ—by making itself responsible for the cause of the State. And so, with its political judgments and choices, it bears an implicit, indirect, but none the less real witness to the gospel.

Even its political activity is therefore a profession of its Christian faith. By its political activity it calls the State from neutrality, ignorance, and paganism into co-responsibility before God, thereby remaining faithful to its own particular mission. It sets in motion the historical process whose aim and content are the moulding of the State into the likeness of the Kingdom of God and hence the fulfilment of the State's own righteous purposes.

XV

The Church is based on the knowledge of the one eternal God, who as such became man and thereby proved Himself a neighbor to man, by treating him with compassion (Luke 10:36 f.). The inevitable consequence is that in the political sphere the Church will always and in all circumstances be interested primarily in human beings and not in some abstract cause or other, whether it be anonymous capital or the State as such (the functioning of its departments!) or the honour of the nation or the progress of civilisation or culture or the idea, however conceived, of the historical development of the human race. It will not be interested in this last idea even if "progress" is interpreted as meaning the welfare of future generations, for the attainment of which man, human dignity, human life in the present age are to be trampled underfoot. Right itself becomes wrong (*summum ius summa iniuria*) when it is allowed to rule as an abstract form, instead of serving the limitation and hence the preservation of man. The Church is at all times and in all circumstances the enemy of the idol Juggernaut. Since God Himself became man, man is the measure of all things, and man can and must only be used and, in certain circumstances, sacrificed, for man. Even the most wretched man—not man's egoism, but man's humanity—must be resolutely defended against the autocracy of every mere "cause." Man has not to serve causes; causes have to serve man.

XVI

The Church is witness of the divine justification, that is, of the act in which God in Jesus Christ established and confirmed His original claim to man and hence man's claim against sin and death. The future for which the Church waits is the definitive revelation of this divine justification. This means that the Church will always be found where the order of the State is based on a commonly acknowledged law, from submission to which no one is exempt, and which also provides equal protection for all. The Church will be found where all political activity is in all circumstances regulated by this law. The Church always stands for the constitutional State, for the maximum validity and application of that twofold rule (no exemption from and full protection by the law), and therefore it will always be against any degeneration of the constitutional State into tyranny or anarchy. The Church will never be found on the side of anarchy or tyranny. In its politics it will always be urging the civil community to treat this fundamental purpose of its existence with the utmost seriousness: the limiting and the preserving of man by the quest for and the establishment of law.

XVII

The Church is witness of the fact that the Son of man came to seek and to save the lost. And this implies that—casting all false impartiality aside—the Church must concentrate first on the lower and lowest levels of human society. The poor, the socially and economically weak and threatened, will always be the object of its primary and particular concern, and it will always insist on the State's special responsibility for these weaker members of society. That it will bestow its love on them, within the framework of its own task (as part of its service), is one thing and the most important thing; but it must not concentrate on this and neglect the other thing to which it is committed by its political responsibility: the effort to achieve such a fashioning of the law as will make it impossible for "equality before the law" to become a cloak under which strong and weak, independent and dependent, rich and poor, employers and employees, in fact receive different treatment at its hands: the weak being unduly restricted, the strong unduly protected. The Church must stand for social justice in the political sphere. And in choosing between the various socialistic possibilities (social-liberalism? co-operativism? syndicalism? free trade? moderate or radical Marxism?) it will always choose the movement from which it can expect the greatest measure of social justice (leaving all other considerations on one side).

XVIII

The Church is the fellowship of those who are freely called by the Word of grace and the Spirit and love of God to be the children of God. Translated into political terms, this means that the Church affirms, as the basic right which every citizen must be guaranteed by the State, the

173

freedom to carry out his decisions in the politically lawful sphere, according to his own insight and choice, and therefore independently, and the freedom to live in certain spheres (the family, education, art, science, religion, culture), safeguarded but not regulated by law. The Church will not in all circumstances withdraw from and oppose what may be practically a dictatorship, that is, a partial and temporary limitation of these freedoms, but it will certainly withdraw from and oppose any out-and-out dictatorship such as the totalitarian State. The adult Christian can only wish to be an adult citizen, and he can only want his fellow citizens to live as adult human beings.

XIX

The Church is the fellowship of those who, as members of the one Body of the one Head, are bound and committed to this Lord of theirs and therefore to no other. It follows that the Church will never understand and interpret political freedom and the basic law which the State must guarantee to the individual citizen other than in the sense of the basic duty of responsibility which is required of him. (This was never made particularly clear in the classic proclamations of so-called "human rights" in America and France.) The citizen is responsible in the whole sphere of his freedom, political and non-political alike. And the civil community is naturally responsible in the maintenance of its freedom as a whole. Thus the Christian approach surpasses both individualism and collectivism. The Church knows and recognises the "interest" of the individual and of the "whole," but it resists them both when they want to have the last word. It subordinates them to the being of the citizen, the being of the civil community before the law, over which neither the individuals nor the "whole" are to hold sway, but which they are to seek after, to find, and to serve —always with a view to limiting and preserving the life of man.

XX

As the fellowship of those who live in one faith under one Lord on the basis of a Baptism in one Spirit, the Church must and will stand for the equality of the freedom and responsibility of all adult citizens, in spite of its sober insight into the variety of human needs, abilities, and tasks. It will stand for their equality before the law that unites and binds them all, for their equality in working together to establish and carry out the law, and for their equality in the limitation and preservation of human life that it secures. If, in accordance with a specifically Christian insight, it lies in the very nature of the State that this equality must not be restricted by any differences of religious belief or unbelief, it is all the more important for the Church to urge that the restriction of the political freedom and responsibility not only of certain classes and races but, supremely, of that of women is an arbitrary convention which does not deserve to be preserved any longer. If Christians are to be consistent there can be only one possible decision in this matter.

XXI

Since the Church is aware of the variety of the gifts and tasks of the one Holy Spirit in its own sphere, it will be alert and open in the political sphere to the need to separate the different functions and "powers"—the legislative, executive, and judicial—inasmuch as those who carry out any one of these functions should not carry out the others simultaneously. No human being is a god able to unite in his own person the functions of the legislator and the ruler, the ruler and the judge, without endangering the sovereignty of the law. The "people" is no more such a god than the Church is its own master and in sole possession of its powers. The fact is that within the community of the one people (by the people and for the people) definite and different services are to be performed by different persons, which, if they were united in one human hand, would disrupt rather than promote the unity of the common enterprise. With its awareness of the necessity that must be observed in this matter, the Church will give a lead to the State.

XXII

The Church lives from the disclosure of the true God and His revelation, from Him as the Light that has been lit in Jesus Christ to destroy the works of darkness. It lives in the dawning of the day of the Lord and its task in relation to the world is to rouse it and tell it that this day has dawned. The inevitable political corollary of this is that the Church is the sworn enemy of all secret policies and secret diplomacy. It is just as true of the political sphere as of any other that only evil can want to be kept secret. The distinguishing mark of the good is that it presses forward to the light of day. Where freedom and responsibility in the service of the State are one, whatever is said and done must be said and done before the ears and eyes of all, and the legislator, the ruler, and the judge can and must be ready to answer openly for all their actions—without thereby being necessarily dependent on the public or allowing themselves to be flurried. The statecraft that wraps itself up in darkness is the craft of a State which, because it is anarchic or tyrannical, is forced to hide the bad conscience of its citizens or officials. The Church will not on any account lend its support to that kind of State.

XXIII

The Church sees itself established and nourished by the free Word of God—the Word which proves its freedom in the Holy Scriptures at all times. And in its own sphere the Church believes that the human word is capable of being the free vehicle and mouthpiece of this free Word of God.

By a process of analogy, it has to risk attributing a positive and constructive meaning to the free human word in the political sphere. If it trusts the word of man in one sphere it cannot mistrust it on principle in the other. It will believe that human words are not bound to be empty or useless or even dangerous, but that the right words can clarify and control great decisions. At the risk of providing opportunities for empty, useless, and dangerous words to be heard, it will therefore do all it can to see that there is at any rate no lack of opportunity for the *right* word to be heard. It will do all it can to see that there are opportunities for mutual discussion in the civil community as the basis of common endeavours. And it will try to see that such discussion takes place openly. With all its strength it will be on the side of those who refuse to have anything to do with the regimentation, controlling, and censoring of public opinion. It knows of no pretext which would make that a good thing and no situation in which it could be necessary.

XXIV

As disciples of Christ, the members of His Church do not rule: they serve. In the political community, therefore, the Church can only regard all ruling that is not primarily a form of service as a diseased and never as a normal condition. No State can exist without the sanction of power. But the power of the good State differs from that of the bad State as *potestas* differs from *potentia*. *Potestas* is the power that follows and serves the law; *potentia* is the power that precedes the law, that masters and bends and breaks the law—it is the naked power which is directly evil. Bismarck—not to mention Hitler—was (in spite of the *Daily Bible Readings* on his bedside table) no model statesman because he wanted to establish and develop his work on naked power. The ultimate result of this all-too-consistently pursued aim was inevitable: "all that draw the sword shall perish by the sword." Christian political theory leads us in the very opposite direction.

XXV

Since the Church is ecumenical (catholic) by virtue of its very origin, it resists all abstract local, regional, and national interests in the political sphere. It will always seek to serve the best interests of the particular city or place where it is stationed. But it will never do this without at the same time looking out beyond the city walls. It will be conscious of the superficiality, relativity, and temporariness of the immediate city boundaries, and on principle it will always stand for understanding and cooperation within the wider circle. The Church will be the last to lend its support to mere parochial politics. *Pacta sunt servanda? Pacta sunt concludenda!* All cities of the realm must agree if their common cause is to enjoy stability and not fall to pieces. In the Church we have tasted the air of freedom and must bring others to taste it, too.

XXVI

The Church knows God's anger and judgment, but it also knows that His anger lasts but for a moment, whereas His mercy is for eternity. The political analogy of this truth is that violent solutions of conflicts in the political community —from police measures to law court decisions, from the armed rising against a regime that is no longer worthy of or equal to its task (in the sense of a revolt undertaken not to undermine but to restore the lawful authority of the State) to the defensive war against an external threat to the lawful State—must be approved, supported, and if necessary even suggested by the Christian community—for how could it possibly contract out in such situations? On the other hand, it can only regard violent solutions of any conflict as an *ultima ratio regis.* It will approve and support them only when they are for the moment the ultimate and only possibility available. It will always do its utmost to postpone such moments as far as possible. It can never stand for absolute peace, for peace at any price. But it must and will do all it can to see that no price is considered too high for the preservation or restoration of peace at home and abroad except the ultimate price which would mean the abolition of the lawful State and the practical denial of the divine ordinance. May the Church show her inventiveness in the search for other solutions before she joins in the call for violence! The perfection of the Father in heaven, who does not cease to be the heavenly Judge, demands the earthly perfection of a peace policy which really does extend to the limits of the humanly possible.

XXVII

These are a few examples of Christian choices, decisions, and activities in the political sphere: examples of analogies and corollaries of that Kingdom of God in which the Church believes and which it preaches, in the sphere of the external, relative, and provisional problems of the civil community. The translation of the Kingdom of God into political terms demands Christian, spiritual, and prophetic knowledge on every side. The points of comparison and the decisions we have quoted are in no sense equivalent to the paragraphs of a political constitution. They are merely intended to illustrate how the Church can make decisions on a Christian basis in the political sphere. We might have taken twice or three times as many or only half as many examples or just one example to make the vital point clear. We used examples because we were concerned to illuminate the analogical but extremely concrete relationship between the Christian gospel and certain political decisions and modes of behaviour. The only more concrete way of discussing the relationship would be to refer to individual historical decisions. The reason why we mentioned many examples

was that we wanted to demonstrate that the essence of
Christian politics is not a system or a succession of momen-
tary brain waves but a constant direction, a continuous line
of discoveries on both sides of the boundary which separates
the political from the spiritual spheres, a correlation between explication and application. The list of such explications and applications that we have offered here is naturally
incomplete. And it is of the very nature of all such points
of contact and decision as have been or could have been
mentioned that the translations and transitions from the one
sphere to the other will always be open to discussion as far
as the details are concerned, will only be more or less obvious and never subject to absolute proof. What we have
said here needs to be extended, deepened, and particular-
ised. The more one studies the problems of translation from
one sphere to the other, the more one will realise that it is
not possible to deal with every problem in this way. But the
clarity of the message of the Bible will guarantee that all
the explications and applications of the Christian approach
will move in one unswerving direction and one continuous
line. What we were concerned to show was the possibility
and the necessity of comparisons and analogies between the
two spheres and of the decisions which have to be made
in the transition from one to the other.

XXVIII

Let me add a comment on the constancy and continuous-
ness of the line of Christian political thought and action that
we have indicated. We have argued not from any conception of "natural law" but from the gospel. It cannot be denied, however, that in the list of examples quoted we have
more than once made assertions which have been justified
elsewhere on the basis of natural law. We bear no grudge
against anyone who may have been reminded of Rousseau
—and who may have been pleased or angry on that account. We need not be ashamed of the affinity. We have

seen that the divine ordinance of the State makes it perfectly possible for theoretical and practical insights and decisions to be reached, which are objectively right, where one would inevitably expect only errors and false steps, in view of the turbid source from which they derive. If our results really did coincide with theses based on natural law, it would merely confirm that the *polis* is in the Kingdom of Jesus Christ even when its officeholders are not aware of the fact or refuse to admit it, and therefore are unable to use the insight into the nature of the *polis* which this fact suggests. Why should it be impossible that, in spite of the State's blindness, objectively correct insights have been and are being reached again and again? The pagan State lives because such leadership of the blind has repeatedly made its stability and its functions possible. All the more reason, surely, why the Church cannot and must not withhold its witness to an insight based on clearly defined and consistently applicable facts.

XXIX

A further comment on the constancy and continuity of the Christian approach in politics: it may be remarked (again, with pleasure or annoyance) that the Christian line that follows from the gospel betrays a striking tendency to the side of what is generally called the "democratic" State. Here again, we shall be careful not to deny an obvious fact, though "democracy" in any technical meaning of the word (Swiss, American, French, etc.), is certainly not necessarily the form of State closest to the Christian view. Such a State may equally well assume the form of a monarchy or an aristocracy, and occasionally even that of a dictatorship. Conversely, no democracy as such is protected from failing in many or all of the points we have enumerated and degenerating not only into anarchy but also into tyranny and thereby becoming a bad State. It must be admitted that the word and the concept "democracy" ("the rule of the people") are powerless to describe even approximately the kind of State which, in the Christian view, most nearly corresponds to the divine ordinance. This is no reason, however, why it should be overlooked or denied that Christian choices and purposes in politics tend on the whole towards the form of State, which, if it is not actually realised in the so-called "democracies," is at any rate more or less honestly clearly intended and desired. Taking everything into account, it must be said that the Christian view shows a stronger trend in this direction than in any other. There certainly is an affinity between the Christian community and the civil communities of the free peoples.

XXX

In conclusion, we propose to discuss the problem of how Christian decisions in the political sphere may be put into action.

The first method that suggests itself is the formation and activity of a special Christian party. This has long been adopted in Holland and later in Switzerland (Evangelical People's Party), and in recent times especially in France (Mouvement Républicain Populaire) and Germany (Christian Democratic Union). On the Protestant side it has been deemed possible and necessary to join forces with Roman Catholic fellow citizens with the same political views. But parties are one of the most questionable phenomena in political life: they are in no sense its constitutive elements, and it is possible that from the very outset they have been pathological or at least no more than secondary phenomena. I wonder if the Christian community is well advised to add one more to the number of these organisations in order to fulfil its own share of political responsibility? Can there be any other "Christian" party in the State but the Christian fellowship itself, with its special mission and purpose? And if what we want is a political corollary of the Church in political life, can anything else be permissible and possible

but—please do not be scared!—a single State party excluding all others, whose programme would necessarily coincide with the tasks of the State itself, understood in the
widest sense (but excluding all particularist ideas and interests)? How can there be a special Christian party alongside other political parties?—a party to which some Christians belong, whilst others do not—a party opposed by other
non-Christian parties (which it must nevertheless recognise
as legitimately non-Christian)? To institute special Christian parties implies that the Christian community as such
has no claim on the support of all its members for its own
political line. It implies that it cannot help but allow the
non-Christians in the State to consolidate themselves in a
non-Christian bloc in order to enforce their own anti-
Christian line. The Church's supreme interest must be rather
that Christians shall not mass together in a special party,
since their task is to defend and proclaim, in decisions based
on it, the Christian gospel that concerns all men. They must
show that although they go their own special way, they are
not in fact against anybody but unconditionally for all men,
for the common cause of the whole State.

In the political sphere the Christian community can draw
attention to its gospel only indirectly, as reflected in its political decisions, and these decisions can be made intelligible
and brought to victory not because they are based on Christian premises but only because they are politically better
and more calculated to preserve and develop the common
life. They can witness only to Christian truths. The claim
to be witnesses to Christian truths does not necessarily make
them such, however! Surely it will be inevitable that the
Christian qualities for which it can have no use in the political sphere will become an embarrassment to a Christian
party? And will not the aims and methods which it needs
if it is to be effective as a political party (the winning of
majorities and political strongholds, propaganda and the
benevolent toleration and even encouragement of non-
Christian or problematically Christian sympathisers and

even leaders; compromises and coalitions with "non-Christian" parties and so on) compel it to deny the specifically Christian content of its policy or at any rate obscure rather than illuminate it? Will such a party not inevitably be compromising the Christian Church and its message all the time? In the political sphere Christians can bring in their Christianity only anonymously. They can break through this anonymity only by waging a political battle for the Church and by so doing they will inevitably bring discredit and disgrace on the Christian name. In the authentically political questions which affect the development of the civil community, Christians can only reply in the form of decisions which could be the decisions of any other citizens, and they must frankly hope that they may become the decisions of all other citizens regardless of their religious profession. How can Christians mass together in a political party at all in these circumstances? The thing is only possible—and the suspicious alliance of the Protestants with the Romans in the French M.R.P. and the German C.D.U. shows that it becomes successful only where the Kingdom of God is interpreted as a human goal founded on natural law, where an allegedly Christian law, which is in fact a mere amalgam of humanitarian philosophy and morality, is set alongside the gospel in the political sphere. When it is represented by a Christian party, the Christian community cannot be the political salt which it is its duty to be in the civil community.

XXXI

The opportunity that it is offered to fulfil this duty is simply the one that lies nearest to hand: the preaching of the whole gospel of God's grace, which as such is the whole justification of the whole man—including political man. This gospel which proclaims the King and the Kingdom that is now hidden but will one day be revealed is political from the very outset, and if it is preached to real (Christian

and non-Christian) men on the basis of a right interpretation of the Scriptures it will necessarily be prophetically
political. Explications and applications of its political content in an unmistakable direction will inevitably take place
(whether in direct or indirect illumination of the political
problems of the day) where the Christian community is
gathered together in the service of this gospel. Whether
this happens or not will depend on the preachers, but not
only on them. It is a bad sign when Christians are fright-
ened by "political" sermons—as if Christian preaching could
be anything but political. And if it were not political, how
would it show that it is the salt and the light of the world?
The Christian Church that is aware of its political responsibility will demand political preaching; and it will interpret
it politically even if it contains no direct reference to politics. Let the Church concentrate first, however, on seeing
that the whole gospel really is preached within its own area.
Then there will be no danger of the wider sphere beyond
the Church not being wholesomely disturbed by it.

XXXII

The Christian community acts within the meaning and
limits of its own mission and competence when it speaks,
through the mouth of its presbyterial and synodal organs,
in important situations in political life, by making represen-
tations to the authorities or by public proclamations. It will
be careful to select, as wisely as possible, the particular
situations in which it deems it right to speak, and it will
have to choose its words very prudently and very definitely
if it is to be heard. It must not give the impression that it
never wakes from the sleep of an otherwise non-political existence until such matters as gambling or the abuse of al-
cohol or the desecration of the Sabbath or similar questions
of a religious and ethical nature in the narrower sense are
under discussion, as if such problems were not in fact only
on the verge of real political life. The Church must see that

it does not make a habit of coming on the scene too late, of entering the fray only when its opinions no longer involve any particular risk and can no longer exert any particular influence. It must see above all that the idea of the Church as the representative of a definitive class-conditioned outlook and morality is not allowed to gain ground, thereby confirming those who already loyally believe in this "law" and arousing the disapproval of those who are, on the contrary, unable to regard such a "law" as in any sense eternal. All this applies just as much to the Christian journalism and writing that are carried on with or even without the authority of the Church. Christian publicists and writers must place themselves honestly in the service of the gospel which is intended for all men and not devote their gifts to some Christian fad or another.

XXXIII

Perhaps the most important contribution the Church can make is to bear in mind in the shaping of its own life that, gathered as it is directly and consciously around the common centre, it has to represent the inner within the outer circle. The real Church must be the model and prototype of the real State. The Church must set an example so that by its very existence it may be a source of renewal for the State and the power by which the State is preserved. The Church's preaching of the gospel would be in vain if its own existence, constitution, order, government, and administration were not a practical demonstration of the thinking and acting from the gospel which takes place in this inner circle. How can the world believe the gospel of the King and His Kingdom if by its own actions and attitudes the Church shows that it has no intention of basing its own internal policy on the gospel? How can a reformation of the whole people be brought about if it is common knowledge that the Church itself is bent only on self-preservation and restoration—or not even that? Of the political implications of theology which we have enumerated, there are few which do not merit attention first of all in the life and development of the Church itself. So far they have not received anything like enough attention within the Church's own borders.

What nonsense it is, for example, that in a country like Germany which has diligently to learn the rudiments of law, freedom, responsibility, equality, and so on, that is, the elements of the democratic way of life, the Church considers it necessary to act more and more hieratically and bureaucratically and becomes a refuge for nationalism in a situation in which it ought supremely to appear as the holy catholic Church, and thereby help to lead German politics out of an old defile. The Church must not forget that what it is rather than what it says will be best understood, not least in the State.

XXXIV

If the Church is a Christian community it will not need a Christian party. If it is a true fellowship it will perform with its words and its whole existence all the functions which the disastrous enterprise of "Christian" parties is evidently intended to fulfil. There will be no lack of individual Christians who will enter the political arena anonymously, that is, in the only way they can appear on the political scene, and who will act in accordance with the Christian approach and will thereby prove themselves unassuming witnesses of the Gospel of Christ, which can alone bring salvation in the political sphere no less than elsewhere. Any fame that they acquire will not be founded on the fact that they are "nice, pious people" but simply that from their own distinctive point of view they will know better than others what is best for the civil community. It is not the presence and co-operation of "Christian personalities" that helps the State. One thinks of Bismarck again: assuming for the moment that he was something like the "Christian personality" that legend describes him to have been, what difference did it make to the unfortunate tendency of his politics? What help was it to poor Germany? The way Christians can help in the political sphere is by constantly giving the State an impulse in the Christian direction and freedom to develop on the Christian line. Let it not be said that there are too few of such Christians and that these few in their isolation are helpless. How much one individual can do whose heart and soul are really wrapped up in the cause! And in any case Christians are not asked to do something in their own strength, but only what they are required to do by the grace of God.

What does it matter if they are isolated and if—since there are such things as parties—they are members of different parties, that is, of one of the various "non-Christian" parties? They will take the party programme, party discipline, party victories, and party defeats in which they are involved as seriously and humorously as the cause deserves. In every party they will be against narrow party policies and stand up for the interests of the whole community. By that token they will be political men and women in the primary meaning of the word. Scattered in different places, and known or unknown to one another, in touch with one another or out of touch, they will all be together—as citizens —and will make the same distinctions and judgments, choose and desire one cause, work for one cause. Let us pray that the Church may supply the State with such Christians, such citizens, such political men and women in the primary meaning of the word! For in their existence the Church will be fulfilling its share of political responsibility in the most direct form.

XXXV

Let me remind you once again of the fifth thesis of the *Theological Declaration* of Barmen, which I have quoted from several times already: "The Bible tells us that, in accordance with a divine ordinance, the State has the task of providing for law and peace in the world that still awaits redemption, in which the Church stands, according to the measure of human insight and human capacity, and upheld by the threat and use of force. The Church acknowledges the benefaction of this divine ordinance with a thankful, reverent heart. It reminds men of God's Kingdom, God's Commandment and justice, and thereby of the responsibility of governors and governed alike. It trusts and obeys the power of the Word by which God sustains all things."

I think that I have dealt with "The Christian Community and the Civil Community" within the terms of this thesis, and therefore in accordance with the mind of the Confessional Church in Germany. Some things would be different now if that Church had itself given more attention to this section of the Declaration in good time. But it cannot be too late to return to it now with a new seriousness, deepened and strengthened by experience.

SELECTED BIBLIOGRAPHY

(This list includes the chief writings of Karl Barth available in English, directly relevant to the questions raised in the three essays included in this volume. In every case, there is indication of the date and manner of original publication.)

THEOLOGICAL EXISTENCE TODAY! London: Hodder and Stoughton, 1933 (*Theologische Existenz heute!* Munich: Chr. Kaiser Verlag, 1933. *Theologische Existenz heute! No. I*).

TROUBLE AND PROMISE IN THE STRUGGLE OF THE CHURCH IN GERMANY. Oxford: Clarendon Press, 1938 (*Not und Verheissung im deutschen Kirchenkampf.* Bern: BEG-Verlag, 1938).

THE KNOWLEDGE OF GOD AND THE SERVICE OF GOD ACCORDING TO THE REFORMATION (Gifford Lectures). London: Hodder and Stoughton, 1938 (*Gotteserkenntnis und Gottesdienst.* Zollikon-Zurich: Evangelischer Verlag, 1938).

CHURCH AND STATE. London: S.C.M. Press, 1939 (*Rechtfertigung und Recht.* Zollikon-Zurich: Evangelischer Verlag, 1938. *Theologische Studien No. I*).

THE CHURCH AND THE POLITICAL PROBLEM OF OUR DAY. London, Hodder and Stoughton, 1939. ("Die Kirche und die politische Frage von heute" [1938], in Karl Barth, *Eine Schweizer Stimme, 1938–1945.* Zollikon-Zurich: Evangelischer Verlag, 1945.)

THIS CHRISTIAN CAUSE. New York: Macmillan, 1941. Containing: "First Letter to the French Protestants" (December 1939); "Second Letter to the French Protestants" (October 1940); and "A Letter to Great Britain from Switzerland" (April 1941). ("Ein Brief nach Frankreich" [1939]; "Eine Frage und eine Bitte an die Protestanten in Frankreich" [1940]; and "Ein Brief aus der Schweiz nach Grossbritannien" [1941]: all in Karl Barth, *Eine Schweizer Stimme, 1938–1945.* Zollikon-Zurich: Evangelischer Verlag, 1945.)

"A Letter to American Christians," *Christendom,* Vol. VIII (1943), pp. 441–58. ("Brief an einen amerkanischen Kirchenmann" [1942], in Karl Barth, *Eine Schweizer Stimme, 1938–1945.* Zollikon-Zurich: Evangelischer Verlag, 1945.)

THE ONLY WAY. New York: Philosophical Library, 1947. Containing: "How Can the Germans Be Cured?"; "Letters"; "The Germans and Ourselves." (*Wie können die Deutschen gesund werden?* Zollikon-Zurich: Evangelischer Verlag, 1945, and in *Eine Schweizer Stimme, 1938–1945.* Zollikon-Zurich: Evangelischer Verlag, 1945; "Zwei Briefwechsel" [April, 1945], in *Eine Schweizer Stimme, 1938–1945.* Zollikon-Zurich: Evangelischer Verlag, 1945; *Die Deutschen und Wir.* Zollikon-Zurich: Evangelischer Verlag, 1945, and in *Eine Schweizer Stimme, 1938–1945.* Zollikon-Zurich: Evangelischer Verlag, 1945.)

AGAINST THE STREAM: SHORTER POST-WAR WRITINGS, 1946–1952. New York: Philosophical Library, 1954. Containing (among others): "The Christian Community and the Civil Community"; "The Christian Community in the Midst of Political Change: Documents of an Hungarian Journey"; "The Church Between East and West"; "Political Decisions in the Unity of Faith"; and "The Christian Message in Europe Today." (*Christengemeinde und Bürgergemeinde.* Zollikon-Zurich: Evangelischer Verlag, 1946; *Christliche Gemeinde im Wechsel der Staatsordnungen: Dokumente einer*

Ungarnreise. Zollikon-Zurich: Evangelischer Verlag, 1948; *Die Kirche zwischen Ost und West.* Zollikon-Zurich: Evangelischer Verlag, 1949; *Politische Entscheidung in der Einheit des Glaubens.* Munich: Chr. Kaiser Verlag, 1952. *Theologische Existenz heute* [new series] No. 34; *Die christliche Botschaft in heutigen Europa.* Munich: Chr. Kaiser Verlag, 1946. *Theologische Existenz heute* [new series] No. 3.)

HOW TO SERVE GOD IN A MARXIST LAND. New York: Association Press, 1959. Contains: "Letter to a Pastor in the German Democratic Republic." (*Brief an einen Pfarrer in der DDR.* Zollikon-Zurich: Evangelischer Verlag, 1958.)

(A good deal of relevant material is to be found in *The Word of God and the Word of Man* [Boston: Pilgrim Press, 1928; Harper Torchbooks, 1958]; *The Epistle to the Romans* [London: Oxford University Press, 1933]; and *Church Dogmatics* [Edinburgh: T. and T. Clark, 1936 to date].)